NEWFOUNDLAND'S LAST PRIME MINISTER

NEWFOUNDLAND'S LAST PRIME MINISTER

Frederick Alderdice and the Death of a Nation

DOUG LETTO

BOULDER
PUBLICATIONS

Library and Archives Canada Cataloguing in Publication

Letto, Doug, 1958-, author
    Newfoundland's last Prime Minister : Frederick Alderdice and the death of a nation / Doug Letto.

ISBN 978-1-927099-45-2 (pbk.)

    1. Alderdice, F. C. (Frederick Charles) 1872-1936. 2. Prime ministers--Newfoundland and Labrador--Biography. 3. Businessmen--Newfoundland and Labrador--Biography. 4. Newfoundland and Labrador--Politics and government--1855-1934. 5. Newfoundland and Labrador--Biography. I. Title.

FC2173.1.A53L47 2014   971.8'02   C2014-905183-2

Published by Boulder Publications
Portugal Cove-St. Philip's, Newfoundland and Labrador
www.boulderpublications.ca

Editor: Stephanie Porter
Copy editor: Iona Bulgin
Interior design and layout: Alison Carr
Cover design: John Andrews

Printed in Canada

We acknowledge the financial support of the Government of Newfoundland and Labrador through the Department of Tourism, Culture and Recreation.

We acknowledge the financial support for our publishing program by the Government of Canada and the Department of Canadian Heritage through the Canada Book Fund.

For Joan, Aimee, and Doug Brien

TABLE OF CONTENTS

INTRODUCTION

Newfoundland was in a tough spot in 1932. The banks refused to lend the government any more money, and political leaders were fast running out of options to meet their financial obligations. The Squires government, elected in 1928, had been turfed from office by an angry, and increasingly cash-strapped, populace.

The new prime minister was Frederick Alderdice, a local businessman who had advanced through a family-run St. John's rope and twine manufacturing firm. Alderdice's United Newfoundland Party (UNP) was made up mostly of businessmen, lawyers, and other professionals who campaigned on a promise to create employment[1] and reduce taxation.[2] Those promises would prove extraordinarily difficult. Squires and the outgoing government had found a way to make the mid-year debt payment of $2.5 million, but that money had not come easily, and the challenge of making the debt payment would be faced again six months later.

Alderdice and his ministers, trying to find a way out of the financial mess, cut general government spending, including salaries and pensions, increased duties on some items, and introduced duties on essential supplies such as flour. In the fall of 1932, just a

---

1 *Evening Telegram*, May 14, 1932.
2 Ibid., May 28, 1932.

few months after taking office, Alderdice made a radical suggestion—partial default, where Newfoundland would pay only part of the interest due on its bonds. An enraged British government rejected the idea, reminding Alderdice that no part of the British Empire had ever defaulted on a debt commitment, and that Newfoundland would most certainly not be the first to do so. Alderdice capitulated, and struck a deal: if Britain and Canada would help cover Newfoundland's December 31 debt payment, Alderdice would agree to a royal commission to study Newfoundland's affairs.

The Amulree Royal Commission concluded that party politics had ruined Newfoundland and that the population needed a break. In return for Newfoundland's giving up self-government in favour of an appointed commission of government, Britain would cover Newfoundland's budget shortfalls until 1936. Furthermore, Britain would lessen the strain on the island's Treasury by reducing the interest on its bonds by nearly half. Investors were comforted that the bonds would be fully backed by Great Britain. Alderdice and his party, who controlled 25 of the legislature's 27 seats, readily agreed. The appointed Legislative Council concurred, and in November 1933 Newfoundland ended 80 years of elected government.

Alderdice has been described by some as a minor figure in Newfoundland political history, a man who stood in the shadow of political giants like Bond, Morris, and Squires.

But could Alderdice have played a larger role by helping Newfoundland keep the right to run its own affairs? Why didn't he take a stand when the British fought his partial default proposal? Why did only a few members of the public and the two-member Liberal Opposition object to giving up Newfoundland's independence?

This book traces the political change that brought Alderdice to power, his attempts to put public finances in order, and his capitulation to the wishes of Britain's political leaders. Alderdice was leader at a pivotal moment in Newfoundland history. When the opportunity arose for him to be courageous and to step out of the shadow of Bond, Morris, and Squires, he blinked. By agreeing to suspend democratic government in Newfoundland, Alderdice and his supporters led Newfoundland into uncertain constitutional territory, allowing Canada and Britain to direct Newfoundland toward Confederation in 1949.

CHAPTER 1

Second Time Lucky

The summer of 1932 started perfectly, with warm days, light winds from the west and southwest, and long hours of sunlight. St. John's was alive with the sounds of children, out of school for the summer. Senior students, wanting to go on to university in Canada, the United States, or the United Kingdom, were writing entrance exams. Optimistic storeowners advertised children's swimsuits. Auctioneers carried out live animal auctions. Shipping lines advertised passages to exotic London, New York, Boston, and Montreal. Arctic explorer and navigator Captain Bob Bartlett stopped at his home port of Brigus to take on building supplies before heading to northern Greenland to build a memorial to Admiral Robert Peary, the American who claimed to have been the first to reach the North Pole. Capelin and cod were abundant but, according to reports from Placentia Bay, lying lazily near the bottom: "What is needed is a breeze of wind to stir up the fish and make them take bait."[3]

Anyone who dared look deeper, however, would see long-standing problems and gripes lurking beneath the idyllic sights and

---

3 *Daily News*, June 23, 1932.

Members of the last Newfoundland House of Assembly. Front row (left to right): Kenneth M. Brown; William C. Winsor; William J. Walsh; John C. Puddester; F. Gordon Bradley; James A. Winter; Frederick C. Alderdice; Edward Emerson; John G. Stone; William J. Browne; Harry A. Winter; Samuel J. Foote; and Harold Mitchell. Middle row (left to right): Ernest Gear; Phillip J. Lewis, William A. Abbott; page; sergeant-at-arms; Patrick K. Devine (assistant clerk); Michael A. Shea; Herman W. Quinton; Charles J. Furey; Dr. Harris M. Mosdell; and Gerald G. Byrne. Back row (left to right): George Whiteley; Patrick F. Halley; Henry Y. Mott (clerk); Henry Earle; Norman Gray; Joseph Moore; and Roland G. Starkes. *Archives and Special Collections, Queen Elizabeth II Library, Memorial University of Newfoundland (ASC), Coll-075, 5.05.216*

sounds of early summer. A letter writer to the *Daily News* complained that railway officials had the nerve to ask the public to "Be a Booster" to the rail service but could not keep the trains running.[4] A crowd of unemployed men on Bell Island threatened to break into the government's relief stores if they did not get more dole.[5] The *Daily News* editor lamented that the poor state of roads in St. John's and nearby communities was negatively impacting the economy.[6]

And then there was politics. The Liberals had been soundly

---

4 Ibid.

5 Ibid., June 28, 1932.

6 *Evening Telegram*, June 25, 1932.

trounced by the conservative UNP on June 11, but Liberal prime minister Sir Richard Squires was not in a hurry to move on. "The country is beginning to ask when the defeated government proposes to hand in their resignation," wrote the *Daily News* editor. "So let them get out quickly and give place to men of the people's choice."[7] The *Evening Telegram* referred to Squires and his administration as the "defunct Government," and called on them to leave: "There are but three days to the end of the fiscal year and it is imperative that the Alderdice Government assume their responsibilities at once."[8]

No matter which party was in charge, the chief problem facing the government was its finances. Interest payments on the national debt approached a crippling $5 million a year, half of which was due at the end of June, the other half at the end of December. Canadian banks had stopped lending to Newfoundland as of the end of 1931 and so, in the spring of 1932, Squires and his ministers decided to raise a "Prosperity Loan" of $2.5 million within Newfoundland. They found most of that amount by granting Imperial Oil a monopoly on certain fuel sales in Newfoundland in exchange for a loan of $1.75 million. The Anglo-Newfoundland Development Company, owners of the paper mill at Grand Falls, pledged $250,000. Squires planned to raise the remainder from the Newfoundland public but fell short by about $150,000, an amount made up by borrowing from the Reparations Fund, Newfoundland's share of Germany's reparations payments from World War I.[9] The *Telegram* donated a full-page advertisement on June 22 promoting the loan subscription drive.

---

7 *Daily News*, June 23, 1932.

8 *Evening Telegram*, June 27, 1932.

9 *Newfoundland Royal Commission Report 1933* (London: His Majesty's Stationery Office, 1934), ch. IV, para. 140. Hereafter *Amulree Report*.

The loan was not fully subscribed by the time Frederick Charles Alderdice's UNP won the June 11 election. Although he was not sworn in as prime minister until late in June, Alderdice promoted the loan by signing his name to an advertisement in the *Daily News*. "You have just expressed by your votes in a manner unprecedented in our history," he wrote, referring to his landslide victory. "I am appealing to you [to help] re-establish credit at home and abroad in Newfoundland finances. It is gilt edged. Your money is absolutely safe. Never was the patriotic appeal stronger than it is now."[10]

The 1932 vote was Alderdice's second attempt to win a general election. In the summer of 1928, Alderdice had taken over the government's leadership from his cousin Walter Stanley Monroe. Alderdice was prime minister for just 10 weeks—then he was soundly defeated in the 1928 election by Squires, who had rebounded from a corruption scandal that had forced him from office in 1923. Alderdice had bided his time as Opposition leader and, as the 1932 election approached, the probability of his taking back the government improved. The Great Depression hit Newfoundland hard, destroying markets for cod and iron ore, and Squires had few options by which to recover and improve the government's precarious fiscal position. Each month brought more unemployed Newfoundlanders and less government revenue. The public debt was crushing and the demand on the public purse remained strong. During the 1932 campaign, Alderdice railed against Squires and his government, concluding with a live radio address from St. John's in which he likened Squires to a disloyal servant who should be dismissed "upon the first available opportunity." He rebutted those, including former UK financial advisor to Newfoundland Sir Percy Thompson, who "hint[ed] vaguely at

---

10 *Daily News*, June 27, 1932.

the possibility of defaulting"[11] on its financial obligations. Either Alderdice believed the country was less vulnerable than Thompson had suggested or he considered it inadvisable to engage in such talk at the moment that he was on the cusp of victory.

The public bought in, and Alderdice's UNP, a coalition of Conservatives and disaffected Liberals, rode to an overwhelming victory, taking 25 of the 27 seats in the legislature.

On June 28 at Government House, 17 days after his victory, Alderdice finally took the oath of office as Newfoundland's prime minister. Officially, the first order of business that day did not involve Alderdice or his newly elected caucus. Protocol required that Squires hold his final Cabinet meeting. One by one the members of the executive arrived at Government House and, at 11 a.m., the people who had run Newfoundland's affairs for four years gathered around the Cabinet table. So much had changed since the day Squires had taken over in October 1928. The public debt had grown by nearly $20 million; the annual deficit had increased to $4 million, double the average for the previous 12 years; and debt payments were up by nearly $1 million a year to $4.73 million. In a frantic and failed attempt to make up the difference, Squires had slashed spending and increased customs duties. The verdict on his tenure had been handed down: he was out of office.

The formalities continued. At 12:30 p.m., Newfoundland's chief justice, William H. Horwood, acting as administrator in the absence of Governor Sir John Middleton, sent for Alderdice and asked him to form a government. Shortly afterward, Alderdice submitted the names of his Cabinet ministers. Horwood approved the list and set 6 p.m. as the time to swear in the new government.

---

11 *Evening Telegram*, June 10, 1932.

A level of civility prevails during a change of government, even in the wake of a bitter election campaign, such as that fought in the spring of 1932. The presence of the Crown is a factor; politicians deal through the monarch's representative rather than with each other. Once Squires tendered his resignation as prime minister, he sent a memorandum asking the administrator "to invite Mr. Frederick C. Alderdice to form a ministry."[12]

The swearing-in ceremony was administered by Horwood, a man with a distinguished career in Newfoundland public life. Before becoming chief justice in 1902, Horwood had articled with Prime Minister James S. Winter, served as Member of the House of Assembly (MHA) for Trinity and Harbour Grace, served in the Whiteway, Greene, and Bond administrations, and had been a member of Newfoundland's 1895 delegation to Ottawa to discuss Confederation with Canada.

Alderdice's Cabinet members were seasoned figures, most with substantial political, legal, and business experience. He would place particular faith in two of the men sworn in on June 28: John C. Puddester and L. Edward Emerson. Puddester began his professional career as an accountant with the Reid Newfoundland Company, the firm that built the Newfoundland Railway. He later served as business manager with the *Daily News* and likely helped ensure that the paper backed Alderdice and the UNP in the1932 election. Puddester was an incumbent Conservative MHA in 1932, having won Bay de Verde by more than 500 votes in 1928. In 1932, he won the new seat of Carbonear-Bay de Verde with 63 per cent of the vote. Alderdice made him secretary of state, responsible for the Department of Health and Welfare and with the authority to

---

12 The Rooms Provincial Archives of Newfoundland and Labrador, GN/9.36, Cabinet Minutes, June 28, 1932.

administer the dole, a program that proved to be a severe test for the new government and a heavy drain on the Dominion's meagre financial resources. Puddester was described by his Cabinet colleague William J. Browne as "particularly well suited" for his new responsibilities, as he had "comprehensive knowledge of the Railway and of every department of the Civil Service."[13]

Emerson, a lawyer from a distinguished legal family that traced its roots back to the Empire Loyalists, was appointed to the Cabinet by Prime Minister Albert Hickman in 1924, but failed to gain a seat in the election that June. Politics was in Emerson's blood, however, and he ran again in 1928, winning Placentia East by 20 votes. The electorate was even kinder in June 1932, returning Emerson to the legislature as one of two members for St. John's East by a margin of nearly 5,600 votes. He became minister of Justice and Attorney General, and served in the position for the remainder of Alderdice's time in power.

The others sworn in to Alderdice's Cabinet that day included St. John's lawyer Harry A. Winter, who won in Harbour Grace; John Stone, a former businessman, manager in the fish business, and minister of Marine and Fisheries during the war years, who won the seat in Trinity North; Samuel Foote, a lawyer and former Liberal who resigned from Squires's Cabinet in 1923 and ran unsuccessfully for Alderdice in 1928, but won in 1932 in Burin; and James A. Ayre of the well-known St. John's business family, who won Port de Grave. William C. Winsor won in Bonavista North and was named minister of Posts and Telegraphs. Former teacher and Fishermen's Protective Union (FPU) employee, Herbert Quinton, was elected in Bonavista and appointed to the

---

13 William J. Browne, *Eighty-four Years a Newfoundlander: Memoirs of William J. Browne* (St. John's, 1981), 204.

ministry of Public Works. Merchant Francis McNamara, a 15-year veteran of the unelected Legislative Council; lawyer William J. Browne, elected in Harbour Main-Bell Island; and war veteran and businessman Harold Mitchell from Trinity South joined the Cabinet as ministers without portfolio. Mitchell, notably, had defeated Squires by nearly 700 votes. Browne regarded Mitchell as "an unusual person of great candour who had a high reputation for personal integrity and moral courage."[14]

The formal act of installing the new government took place at Government House, a building that had been mired in its own overspending controversy a century earlier. Government House was the brainchild of the island's first civil governor, Thomas Cochrane. The grand residence on Military Road had cost a small fortune—£38,175, five times in excess of the estimate. This cost overrun did not go well with officials in London, who retaliated by reducing Cochrane's salary by 30 per cent, from £4,200 to £3,000.

Before Alderdice's first summer in office was over, he and his Cabinet understood the depth of Newfoundland's fiscal predicament. They retaliated with cutbacks and tax increases. Post offices were shuttered and the entire postal and telegraph system placed under review; government workers' salaries were cut, including pay for MHAs, teachers, and judges; pensions were slashed for World War I heroes. Over the next months, the new government set higher import duties for basic foods such as flour, butter, tea, and beef.

Long before 1932, the Newfoundland government had exhibited a tendency to spend more than it could afford—for example, in the $27 million it had paid to build the railway.[15] While Newfoundland

---

14 Ibid.

15 Specifically, $45 million, including associated financing costs and deficits, according to finance minister P.J. Cashin in his April 22, 1931, budget speech.

prided itself on its contribution to World War I, the war debt, including interest and war pensions, had cost the Dominion another $34.5 million. In 1931, when the national debt was $90 million, Squires's finance minister, Peter Cashin, reckoned that the railway and the war were responsible for 80 per cent of that total. In his 1931 budget speech, Cashin had warned that the government could not indefinitely cover the railway deficits, cautioning that the Public Service was "overmanned [and the] time is not far distant when such duplication will have to be eliminated." Cashin had estimated a deficit of nearly $1.5 million for 1931-32, a shortfall that would be covered by even more borrowing. He was, however, optimistic of borrowing "at a more satisfactory figure than hitherto [since Newfoundland's] resources and industries are sounder" than many of her competitors, and that "our intrinsic value is greater perhaps than ever."[16] Cashin's major concern was that departments contain their spending to their budgeted amounts. He never contemplated, or at least never expressed in his speech, that a combination of diminished revenues and increased spending were about to hit with devastating effect.

Alderdice's Cabinet got down to business on June 29. Its first priority was to let the public know that the Squires administration had gone, and with it, the strong odour of corruption and improbity. The Cabinet dismissed several people who had been appointed by Squires, starting with Squires himself as Reparations Commissioner, a position to which he had re-appointed himself the day before the Alderdice ministry took office. Former Squires Cabinet minister Dr. Alex Campbell was dismissed from his position as a government-employed doctor; all government departments employing him were

---

16 *Proceedings of the House of Assembly*, Budget Speech, April 22, 1931, 300. Hereafter *Proceedings*.

informed that he was "to be immediately notified that his services [were] no longer required."[17] Campbell, a close ally of Squires, had been investigated a decade earlier by the Hollis Walker Inquiry for allegations of corruption involving the Squires government.

The doctor on Bell Island, who also acted as the district surgeon, was also dismissed that day, as were the members of the Railway Commission. The sheriff, the superintendent at Her Majesty's Penitentiary, and the cashier at the Government Savings Bank were also fired. Three of the people let go by Alderdice had been former MHAs in Squires's government. Richard Hibbs of Fogo had become superintendent of the penitentiary; James Bindon of St. Mary's, chief examiner of the Customs Office; and W.W. Halfyard of Trinity North, High Sheriff.[18] The previous incumbents of those offices had all been awarded government pensions to make way for the retiring MHAs. The new Cabinet also revoked a retiring allowance for the mail officer on the Labrador steamer, reversing a decision made at Squires's last Cabinet meeting on June 27.

On May 7, the *Telegram* lambasted Squires for appointing his former MHAs: "Persons still capable of doing their duties have been retired on pensions in order to make room for Government members who dare not go back and face the electorate." It was time, it suggested, to be "out with them [the Squires administration], and let them earn a living by the sweat of their brow."[19]

Hibbs and Halfyard had been FPU members of the last legislature and, in their home turf in the northern bays, where union

---

17 The Rooms Provincial Archives of Newfoundland and Labrador, GN/9.36, Cabinet Minutes, June 29, 1932.

18 All three MHAs, elected in 1928, did not contest the 1932 election. Hibbs and Halfyard were members of the FPU and Bindon had been elected as a Liberal in St. Mary's in 1928.

19 *Evening Telegram*, May 7, 1932.

support was strongest, their dismissals were met with disapproval. In Port Union, *The Fishermen's Advocate* called Alderdice's actions "brutal [and] not since the memorable year of 1897, has a Government in this country attempted such a wholesale and discriminate dismissal of public servants in order to make room for political party friends." It also accused Alderdice's government of playing favourites in dismissing the postmaster at Port Union and replacing him with Vincent Guy, "who was so active in the campaign going around with John Stone and speaking at his meetings."[20] It concluded that "Tory rule has always turned out bad, and this lot of hungry, lean rats are acting as bad as all past Tory governments have done—looked after themselves and a few heelers."[21]

Cabinet minister Harry Winter and MHA William Abbott from St. George's, and their appointments as the government's directors to the International and Paper Company at Corner Brook, were also targeted. The *Advocate* writer pointed out that they would be paid $3,000 a year each, and even though the salaries were paid by the company, "the whole is another indication of the old system of giving the spoils of office to the victors at the polls." With the announcement in the spring of 1932 that the FPU would cease to operate as a political party, the paper was without a "natural" party to support, and declared itself "a free lance politically [and pledged to] treat the present Prime Minister and his Government fairly but fearlessly."[22]

Alderdice's decisions were intended to convey a message to a population under severe financial and economic distress: times had changed in Newfoundland politics. But it would take more

---

20 Elected in Trinity North and appointed minister of Fisheries and Marine.

21 *Fishermen's Advocate*, August 10, 1932. Hereafter *Advocate*.

22 Ibid., July 15, 1932.

than the dismissal of Squires's appointees to address the fundamental issues affecting Newfoundland's finances.

At the first Cabinet meeting, Puddester was appointed to head a subcommittee to investigate and reorganize the Department of Posts and Telegraphs "and such other matters that call for attention." In its review of the new Cabinet, *The Newfoundland Quarterly* judged that the former teacher, railway accountant, and *Daily News* business manager was suited for the role.[23] Posts and Telegraphs was one of the few revenue-producing departments, yet it had not come close to paying for itself—in 1930, for example, it took in $615,000 in revenue but required nearly $790,000 in subsidy to maintain its network of post offices and telegraph facilities. That subsidy was nearly two and a half times the amount the government had spent on public health and just $200,000 less than the budget for education.

The *Daily News* and the *Telegram* both supported a tough approach to the Department of Posts and Telegraphs. In its June 30, 1932, editorial, the *Daily News* congratulated Alderdice for his "prompt action ... in setting up a committee ... to investigate one of the most hopeless in public departments." The same day, the *Telegram* pointed out that "dishonesty had been all too prevalent" in the department. It cited numerous cases where letters had disappeared, mail was soggy on arrival, officials were accused of frequently borrowing from the post office till, and IOUs were a major problem. It concluded that the investigation was necessary.

Alderdice appointed former sealing captain William Winsor as minister of Posts and Telegraphs. Winsor, who had gone to the hunt every year since 1903, was first elected to the House of Assembly in 1904 as the MHA for Bay de Verde. He was highly regarded by his

---

23 "The New Government," *Newfoundland Quarterly* 32.1 (July 1932), 25–31.

Cabinet colleague William J. Browne, who believed Winsor's career as a sealing captain would be useful in the government: "We might expect that discipline would be established and maintained in the Post Office under his command."[24] Winsor later revealed some of the abuses alluded to by the newspapers in relation to the St. John's post office, as he defended cuts to the department's budget: "If I find liquor or a part bottle of liquor in the Post Office, [the postal worker] goes out the next day or I go out. It was like a ship without a master [where staff] were ... coming in there as late as 10:30 [and 11:00] and going out at 12:00 p.m., then coming back at 3:00 and going away at 4:00 p.m." Post office staff had little supervision, which created the potential for mail theft. "These people could put what letters they liked in their pockets ... and 90 chances out of 100, the officials there would not know," Windsor stated.[25]

Other early Cabinet decisions demonstrated Alderdice's concern about the province's economic and fiscal position. On July 9, a subcommittee was formed to discuss "the future policy in relation to the question of relief." Signalling the seriousness of the matter, both Alderdice and Secretary of State Puddester were committee members. The ongoing cost of public relief was not the only cause for concern: $1.1 million was still owed to merchants who filled dole orders under the Squires government. The government had to settle the accounts paid out in May and June and some from December 1931. In his quarterly report to the government in London, Middleton noted that the Squires government had badly under-budgeted by allocating a "token figure" of

---

24 Browne, *Eighty-four Years*, 204.

25 James Hiller, ed., *The Debates of the Newfoundland Legislature 1932–1933* (St. John's: Queen's Printer, 2010), June 30, 1933, 2:385.

$50,000 for able-bodied relief.[26]

In his report for the year ending June 30, 1932, the comptroller and auditor general F.C. Berteau advised the new government "to consider very seriously" how much it was prepared to spend on public relief. He had particular concern about the decision by the Squires government to appoint additional relieving officers. "I think it will be found that the appointment of further Relieving Officers has invariably meant **more** expenditure," he wrote, "and this I viewed with alarm[,] the policy which undertook a survey of the Dominion for the purpose of finding those who needed relief."[27]

In its first 10 days in office, the Alderdice government charted its course. It attempted to bury the ghost of Squires by cancelling some of his appointments, displayed urgency in addressing spending, and investigated the depths of the poverty affecting Newfoundlanders. Alderdice's promise to restore both Newfoundland's economy and the fiscal balance in the public treasury, however, would severely test the prime minister and his government.

---

26 The Rooms Provincial Archives of Newfoundland and Labrador, GN/1/1/7, Governor's quarterly report to London, September 30, 1932.

27 Reports of the Comptroller and Auditor General, for the fiscal year ending June 30, 1932 (St. John's: House of Assembly, 1933), 8.

CHAPTER 2

Alderdice's Early Life

Frederick Alderdice's parents, Rachel Monroe and William Alderdice, married in Belfast in 1870. Their marriage produced two sons, Frederick and Norman, but the couple separated when the children were young. William moved to Australia, leaving Rachel to care for the children. In 1886, she and the two boys left Ireland for St. John's, where her brothers Moses, Daniel, and James Harvey Monroe were established in business.

Belfast was in the throes of its first wave of sectarian riots in 1886. British prime minister William Gladstone had failed to get his Irish Home Rule Bill through Parliament, and, while the majority Protestant population in Ireland was relieved, Catholics were worried. Violence erupted in June and continued, sporadically, for several weeks. Hundreds were injured and at least 31 people killed. Rachel decided Belfast was no place to raise a family, certainly not by a single mother. With her sons in tow, she set sail for St. John's. James had never married, and Rachel and her children were a welcome addition to his household on Park Place. Rachel returned regularly to Ireland, but Frederick remained in St. John's to learn the business side of the rope-making enterprise under the tutelage of his uncles.

Newfoundland's population was less than 200,000 when the Alderdices arrived, of which about 28,610 people lived in the capital, St. John's. The main business of the colony was the fishery. In 1884, more than 60,000 men were employed in this industry, bringing in nearly all of the $6.6 million Newfoundland earned from exports that year.[28] The railway, which would contribute to many of Newfoundland's future financial problems, connected St. John's to Harbour Grace, the island's second largest town. A first-class ticket to Harbour Grace from St. John's cost $2.50. Work was under way for a second branch line to Placentia and would be completed by 1888.

As the Alderdices sailed through the Narrows into St. John's harbour, they saw a city which was concentrated around the

A view of St. John's Harbour from the east end, pre-1892. *ASC, Coll-137, 03.01.004*

---

28 David Alexander, "Newfoundland's Traditional Economy and Development to 1934," *Acadiensis* 5.2 (Spring 1976), 56–78.

water, with a skyline dominated by the Anglican Cathedral, completed in 1850, and the Roman Catholic Basilica, completed in 1855. Beyond the upper levels of the harbour was the countryside, with hundreds of farms stretching from Kilbride in the west to Topsail Road and Waterford Bridge Road, extending northeast to Freshwater Valley and Portugal Cove Road, and east to Quidi Vidi Lake and the White Hills. Most farmers grew potatoes, turnip, and cabbage for the local market, which they sold by making frequent trips along well-worn cart paths to the city. Considerable acreage was devoted to hay and other fodder for cattle, and farmers provided the city with milk, butter, and cream.[29]

In St. John's, the mail was picked up twice a day from several free-standing pillar boxes located throughout the city; a letter mailed by 8 a.m. in the spring and summer, and by 9 a.m. in autumn and winter, would be delivered within the city later that same day. St. John's was an active commercial city; schooners arrived from Labrador with their summer catches of cod, and passengers and cargo vessels arrived from Liverpool, Halifax, Boston, and New York. Merchants plied their wares on the front page of the *Evening Telegram*, a paper that had begun publishing seven years earlier. The paper advertised Hamburg and Bristol brick that could be bought from ships just arrived in St. John's; butter from Antigonish, Nova Scotia, was offered by the barrel. As Christmas approached, merchants sold oranges from Spain; fresh fruit from Florida; turkeys, geese, and ducks from Halifax; and flour from New York. Children were enticed with offers of sleds and skates; well-heeled families had the opportunity to buy an organ from the Boston manufacturer

---

29 Robert MacKinnon, "Farming the Rock: The Evolution of Commercial Agriculture around St. John's, Newfoundland, to 1945," *Acadiensis* 20.2 (Spring 1991), 46–56.

Mason and Hamlin. Christmas flowers were sold by the Villa Nova Orphanage at Manuels, and hard-working storeowners like C.C. Fearn kept his store open until 11 p.m. on Christmas Eve.

Alderdice had arrived in the city in which he would marry, raise a family, rise to the top of business and political life, and spend the rest of his life. But it would not be an easy life.

Depending on which story about his youth is correct, Alderdice either received a cut while curling and did not see a doctor for two weeks, during which time infection had set in, or a serious infection developed after he was injured while playing rugby. Regardless of its source, the injury and infection led to serious lifelong health problems. Alderdice's future Commission of Government colleague Sir John Hope Simpson related this account of Alderdice's condition in early 1934:

> He is a *very* sick man ... He has no feet and only one leg. The other was amputated high up as a result of septicaemia owing to a kick at [rugby]. He was a great player. The septicaemia affected the other foot also and that was amputated. Altogether, he had 18 operations to save the leg and foot.[30]

After the injury, Alderdice used crutches for the rest of his life, and by the 1920s, he depended on a driver to take him around St. John's and to his summer home in Topsail. Family history suggests Alderdice had other health problems, and was a Type 2 diabetic. His well-known predilection for alcohol also compromised his health. Hope Simpson reported his colleague Thomas

---

30 Peter Neary, ed., *White Tie and Decorations: Sir John and Lady Hope Simpson in Newfoundland* (University of Toronto Press, 1996), 27.

Lodge's assessment of one of Alderdice's flaws—changing his mind on issues—this way:

> Lodge attributed Alderdice's alleged equivocation to personal weakness: "I expect that when he said this he was on his fifth whiskey—semi-truculent and semi-maudlin. The Commission meets in the morning and 10 a.m. is the hour when few alcoholics have any moral courage left. Certainly, Alderdice hasn't enough then to argue with Hope Simpson, Trentham, or myself. All we get is a sentimental assurance that he is going to the stake with his colleagues."[31]

Alderdice's physical impairment and possible addiction, however, did not interfere with his ascent through the St. John's business and political elite. He advanced first through Colonial Cordage Company, which had been established by his uncle Moses Monroe, who had come to Newfoundland in 1860 at the age of 18. Alderdice was listed as the company's cashier in 1890, accountant in 1898, and sub-manager by 1904. In 1922, he was made a vice-president and managing director. He learned the business side as well as the craft involved in making nets and twines. He even held a small share in the company, which paid him a $12 dividend on July 25, 1889. That was less than one-fifth of 1 per cent of the $7,440 that the company paid out in dividends that year. Then prime minister Sir Richard Thorburn was an investor in the company, as was former prime minister Sir William Whiteway; both were paid $180 in dividends.[32] The few surviving records of

---

31 Ibid., 69.

32 Whiteway had been prime minister when the company was formed and instituted customs protection that benefited the company—a five-year exemption from import duties and a 5 per cent bounty on imported raw materials.

Colonial Cordage, the company's journals for 1889–92, allude to a young Alderdice on the rise within the company. In 1889, the journals indicate he was paid $80 on September 26, another $80 on December 26, and in the spring another $80—suggesting he received that amount quarterly. By September 1890, his pay had been increased to $90 a quarter; a year later he received $110 a quarter.[33] An income of $320 a year could buy considerable goods and supplies in 1889: a copy of the *Telegram* could be bought for 1 cent; James Murray Grocery's Christmas sale offered fresh pork and mutton for 10 cents a pound; St. John and Fennel offered a barrel of flour that was $4 on sale; S.E. Garland advertised "gent's shaving sets" for $2.50 to $5 and walking sticks from 10 cents to $3.

St. John's was rife with political intrigue when the Alderdices arrived. The Reform Party, led by Sir Robert Thorburn, had been elected in the fall of 1885 with a majority government. Almost immediately, Thorburn reneged on his election promise not to compromise with the Catholics and invited several Liberal Catholics into his government. Thorburn's administration faced heavy criticism from the *Telegram* on this issue, which branded the government "a weak and emasculated band of experimentists." Thorburn would lose the next election to Sir William Whiteway.

Confederation had been rebuffed in 1869, but there was talk that union with Canada might again be on the agenda. Canada feared Newfoundland's attempts to reach trade deals with the US would lead to two related problems—it would strengthen Newfoundland's economy and end all chance of confederation, or encourage Newfoundlanders to seek annexation to the US.[34] At

---

33 The Rooms Provincial Archives of Newfoundland and Labrador, MG/847, Journals, Colonial Cordage Company, 1889–1890.

34 S.J.R. Noel, *Politics in Newfoundland* (University of Toronto Press, 1971), 37.

the time Alderdice arrived in St. John's with his mother and brother concerns about important fishing and commercial rights that France possessed on the colony's west coast and northern peninsula, the result of the settlement of the Treaty of Utrecht in 1773, were also running high. Newfoundlanders worried that the island's position would be diminished in a diplomatic solution between Britain and France.

The *Evening Telegram* connected these two issues and called on Newfoundlanders to support the new Whiteway government on the settlement of the French Shore question, and against union with Canada. "There is in this country only one party that the people can trust," intoned an editorial on July 22, 1890, "that is the Liberal Party, the Native Party, the Anti-Confederate Party." It promised that Whiteway "would defend Newfoundlanders against tyrannical immigrants, against Confederate traitors, so, too, it will defend them against French aggressors."[35]

The first recorded instance of any political involvement by Alderdice was during the 1908 general election campaign. Alderdice, in his mid-30s, was part of a group of "young men on the rise" who mobilized to support Sir Edward Patrick Morris and his People's Party (in which "all who work for a living … may join together to work for the common good").[36] Morris had been part of Sir Robert Bond's government as justice minister from 1900 to 1907 but broke away to form the Newfoundland People's Party. Morris and Bond tied with 18 seats each in the November 1908 election. Unable to work together in the House of Assembly, they went to the people again six months later. This time Morris won a

---

35 *Evening Telegram*, July 22, 1890.

36 Patrick O'Flaherty, *Lost Country: The Rise and Fall of Newfoundland, 1843–1933* (St. John's, NL: Long Beach Press, 2005), 241.

majority, taking 26 of the legislature's 36 seats.[37] Bond's opponents included "various interest groups [with] close ties to the Reid Newfoundland Company."[38] The Reids had already fallen out with Bond in 1905 when his government refused to buy their railway and steamship operations. Morris was regarded as politically astute and, while his official reason for breaking with Bond was over the wages being paid to road workers, it was more likely a deft political move to capitalize on Bond's political weakness.[39]

In 1905, Alderdice and Colonial Cordage might have had their own reasons to quarrel with Bond for his fisheries policy and its impact on their profitable business. Bond, smarting after the US Senate derailed negotiations for a reciprocity deal between Newfoundland and the US, retaliated by disrupting American fishing activities on the west coast of Newfoundland. His grand gesture deeply affected many Newfoundland-run enterprises by preventing Americans from hiring local crews or buying fish and, critical to Alderdice and his company, forbidding the Americans from buying local supplies. Bond's goal—to resurrect his failed 1902 trade agreement with US secretary of state John Hay—was laudatory. That deal would have allowed the duty-free entry of many Newfoundland goods into the US in return for various privileges for the American fishing fleet in Newfoundland. In

37 Hiller, "Edward Patrick Morris, 1st Baron Morris," in Historica Canada, accessed July 6, 2014, http://www.thecanadianencyclopedia.ca/en/article/edward-patrick-morris-1st-baron-morris/. Hiller concludes that, in his split with Bond in 1907, Morris had been "urged on by Bond's opponents," and that once he became prime minister, "Morris had no clear policy other than to keep himself in power."

38 Melvin Baker and Peter Neary, "Bond, Sir Robert," in *Dictionary of Canadian Biography*, http://www.biographi.ca/en/bio/bond_robert_15E.html.

39 Hiller, "The Political Career of Robert Bond," in *Twentieth Century Newfoundland: Explorations,* ed. Hiller and Neary (St. John's, NL: Breakwater, 1994), 33–34.

their assessment of Bond's actions, Melvin Baker and Peter Neary state that Bond "had badly overstepped himself" in his 1905 reprisals aimed at the American fishing effort in Newfoundland. Officials from Washington, enraged, contacted their counterparts in London and were able to subvert Bond's pressure tactics.[40] It was only a matter of time before Bond's opponents inside and outside of government calculated a way to challenge him politically.

After his brief political involvement in support of Morris, Alderdice stayed away from politics for nearly 20 years. His main concern was the rope and net manufacturing factory on The Ropewalk[41] in St. John's. Alderdice's name showed up frequently in the Colonial Cordage accounts from his early years in Newfoundland. Various amounts were paid under "sundries," suggesting he ran errands and was repaid for purchases made on his own credit account. The company had done well leading up to the turn of the century, earning a profit of just over $2,000 in 1888; $12,531 in 1890; $22,013 in 1891; and $20,112 in 1892. Soon after, dark clouds descended on the Newfoundland economy and this profitable company felt the repercussions.

Nonetheless, Moses Monroe was a rich man. The establishment of Colonial Cordage Company was an astute move, accomplished with significant help from the government. Although Newfoundland's economy had long been tied to the fishery, prior to 1882 no homegrown producer of nets and twine existed—these products were imported. Armed with an exemption from import duties and a bounty on imported raw materials from the government of Sir Richard Thorburn, Moses and James Monroe, along

---

40 Baker and Neary, "Bond, Sir Robert."

41 The Ropewalk, later known as Ropewalk Lane, got its name from the long, narrow building where fishing ropes were manufactured.

with minority local investors, had built Colonial Cordage into a major business concern. However, their substantial investments in that company and many other enterprises in St. John's were threatened by the bank crash of 1894:

> With the immediate assistance of outside banks, Monroe believed, many of the mercantile firms would indeed be solvent if their owners were given time by their creditors to realize their assets. His suggestion was not generally followed and a large number of firms found themselves placed in trusteeships. Monroe managed to avoid this situation by agreeing with his creditors to pay off his debts in full if permitted sufficient time. This he did, but he nearly depleted his financial resources and saw his health rapidly deteriorate.[42]

Moses Monroe died at the age of 53 in 1895. His estate was valued at just $10,500, but he had managed to save the company he and his brother had built. Four years after the crash, Colonial Cordage had rebounded with $160,000 in paid-up capital, $36,000 more than the profitable years before the bank crash. The healthy balance sheet provided considerable wealth to Moses's wife, Jessie. Her estate was valued at $160,000 when she died in 1906.

Moses Monroe's brother and partner, James Monroe, also profited from the improved fortunes of the company; he left an estate of $270,630 on his death in 1922. Alderdice, an executor of his will, was left James's "two motor cars, carriage, harness and horse, also ... four tenement houses on Pleasant Street which are

---

42 Baker, "Monroe, Moses," Dictionary of Canadian Biography, http://www. biographi.ca/en/bio/monroe_moses_12E.html.

freehold property." James also left 60 per cent of the remainder of his estate to Alderdice and his mother, giving Alderdice the option of converting that interest to shares in Colonial Cordage or Imperial Tobacco Company (Newfoundland). In an addendum to the will just before his death, James left his shares in the Midwest and Gulf Oil Corporations to Alderdice. He left his home at 3 Park Place, with all its contents, to Alderdice's mother. Alderdice's four children were left $5,000 each.

The third Monroe brother in Newfoundland, Daniel Monroe, had an estate worth $197,713 when he died in 1921. He gave $48,000 to various causes and close family members, including $20,000 to his brother William Monroe in New Zealand, and divided the remaining $150,000 equally among 10 people, including his nephew Frederick Alderdice.

Alderdice held directorships with various firms, including Imperial Tobacco Company, which was owned by Walter Monroe. He was a director with the Newfoundland Manufacturers' Mutual Insurance Company, Newfoundland Motor Mutual Assurance Association, and the Eastern Trust Company. Alderdice was part of the city's social elite and held memberships in the Bally Haly Golf Club, City Club, Murray's Pond Fishing Club, British Empire Society, and Overseas Club. A member of the Church of England, he regularly attended St. Thomas' Church on Military Road.

Alderdice's marriage to Harriet Carter on October 25, 1899, reflected the circles in which the St. John's mercantile elite circulated. Harriet traced her lineage at Ferryland to Robert Carter, grandson of the first Carter to land at Ferryland. Robert began accumulating property and wealth in 1750 when he was granted 60 feet of property in a part of Ferryland called The Pool. In the same year, he was appointed Justice of the Peace. His family would include his great-grandson Frederick Carter, a lawyer, who became Conservative prime minister of Newfoundland on two occasions: 1865–70 and 1874–78. Although he was a member of the Church of England, Sir Frederick Carter appointed three Roman Catholics to his first government. He also supported Confederation with Canada and attended the 1864 Quebec Conference as a delegate. He lost the government in 1869 to the anti-Confederates, but returned to a second term as prime minister, after which he became chief justice of the Supreme Court.

Robert Carter's grandson, William, was a judge of the vice-admiralty court during the War of 1812. Although the war was fought primarily in the Great Lakes region of Upper Canada and in the maritime region, Newfoundland raised a regiment of nearly 600 men, who functioned mostly as marines in the Great Lakes campaigns. Newfoundland itself eventually held more than 350 American

Ladies Curling Club, Bally Haly, St. John's, 1939. Harriet Alderdice is standing at the far left, third row from the front. *The Rooms Provincial Archives of Newfoundland and Labrador, 1.13.02.008*

prisoners of war. The end of the War of 1812 affirmed the boundaries of British North America, and Canada and Newfoundland's connection to the British Empire. The continued connection with Britain allowed life to go on as normal in Ferryland. Robert Carter's son Peter became registrar of the court. Another son, James, became sheriff, first of southern Newfoundland, and later, of the entire island; he died in 1925 at the age of 97 with an estate worth $123,241. His niece Harriet and her sisters were left $1,000 each, and Harriet was to share his two-sevenths interest in William Estates,[43] along with five of her sisters and one brother.

Willeen Keough, in her book *The Slender Thread*, which tells the story of Irish Catholic women on the southern Avalon Peninsula, devotes a chapter to Irish and English Protestant women, and draws a picture of the community in which the early Carters lived: "Their husbands, father and brothers … were merchant-planters, mercantile agents, ship owners and captains, naval officers, doctors, and Anglican clerics—men who also served as magistrates and local administrators." In time, "this local gentry … formed the pool from which representatives to the Island's House of Assembly were elected."[44]

In the earliest days of representative government, Robert Carter served as Justice of the Peace and oversaw the election of Ferryland members to the new House of Assembly in St. John's. He opened the polls in Ferryland district for Newfoundland's second general election on November 14, 1836, at 10 a.m. "Large bodies of people assembled from the North & South," he wrote in his diary.

---

43 A St. John's property that had belonged to his maternal uncle, Monier Williams.

44 Willeen Keough, *The Slender Thread: Irish Women on the Southern Avalon, 1750–1860* (Columbia University Press, Electronic Publication Initiative, 2006), ch. 9, *http://www.gutenberg-e.org/keough/kew09.html*.

"People were kept in order" by Reverend J. Duffy, who had paraded through the community the previous day, a Sunday, "with a green flag—his Horses Head stuck with spruce boughs & one in his hand." A Lieutenant R. Carter of the Royal Navy contested a heated election against Patrick Morris. One man "used very tantalizing language against [Carter] ... to create popularity among the crowd—the other party could not be heard at all ..." It seemed all too much for one clergyman, Reverend T. Brown, who "withdrew himself from the Harbour together with his influence ..."[45]

Two weeks after voting started, during which time Robert Carter travelled to Cape Broyle, "Reneuse," Brigus, and Bay Bulls, and four days after Lieutenant R. Carter withdrew from the election, Robert Carter "attended the Court House ... & declared in public the election of Pat'k Morris."[46] The daily entries in Carter's journals describe weather conditions, the passage of vessels north and south of Ferryland, and fish landings, and even suggest he had a role in admitting and clearing vessels that stopped in the harbour. On November 26, 1836, he "measured" the Brig *Aquaforte*, and on September 20, 1852, he permitted "the cattle to be landed to feed [from a vessel that stopped at Ferryland carrying] cattle, 39 sheep—130 packages butter." He also wrote about Sunday services, and his critical observation that one visiting cleric "held church in the forenoon only this day—Mr. Bowman very slack in discharge of his clerical duty."[47]

---

45 Gerald Barnable, Christopher Curran, and Melvin Baker, *A Ferryland Merchant-Magistrate: The Journal and Cases of Robert Carter, Esq., J.P., 1832–1840* (St. John's: Legal-History Committee, The Law Society of Newfoundland and Labrador, 2013), 216.

46 Ibid., 218.

47 Robert Carter, *The Journals of Robert Carter of Ferryland, Newfoundland, 1832–1852*, transcribed and indexed by Jean Carter Stirling, 2002. November 14, 1836.

Harriet Carter, then, was born into Ferryland's ruling family. From Robert and William Carter's beginnings to her grandfather Arthur Hunt O'Brien Carter, who survived near bankruptcy to become a successful businessman, to her own father, William, a customs officer, the Carters were in the thick of Ferryland's and Newfoundland's economic, social, and political life. Keough refers to the Carters and their contemporaries as "middle class [who pressured] their young to enter suitable marriages ... either marrying within their own social circle or recruiting partners from middle-class families in St. John's or areas in England."[48]

The circumstances of Frederick Alderdice and Harriet Carter's meeting and marriage are not known, but it is certain they associated in similar social and economic circles. She travelled frequently to St. John's, and, like Alderdice, she was Anglican. Married life for the Alderdices was comfortable and typical of the upper middle class of the day. It was common for the upper levels of St. John's society to have a summer home, and the Alderdices were no different. They had a place in Topsail, not far from the home of another prominent St. John's businessman, Edgar Hickman. And like most members of their social class, the Alderdices employed a maid to clean house and cook. Summers at Topsail were idyllic, the seashore a playground for their four children and the large and well-developed properties ideal for games and hikes. The family packed up in St. John's when school closed for the summer and did not return until school resumed in September. During the summer, Alderdice and his driver would make the daily 12-mile drive from Topsail to his office at The Ropewalk and back again.

---

48 Keough, *The Slender Thread*, ch. 9.

CHAPTER 3

Prime Minister, for a While

For decades Alderdice had gradually amassed an impressive list of business, professional, and community affiliations and connections, but no political profile beyond his 1908 support of Morris and the People's Party. That changed in 1924 when Walter Monroe became prime minister as leader of the Liberal-Conservatives, a conservative party that brought together St. John's merchants and the working class. Like Alderdice, Monroe had come to Newfoundland from Ireland to work in the family business. Later he started the Monroe Export Company, a fish export firm, and in time became president of the Imperial Tobacco Company.

Monroe appointed Alderdice to the Legislative Council, the unelected upper chamber of the Newfoundland legislature, in 1924. Similar to the Canadian Senate, the Council could not initiate legislation, but it did have the power to defeat or amend it (until 1917, when the House of Assembly removed the Legislative Council's right to defeat legislation that had been approved by the House, leaving the upper chamber with only the power to amend

Bills). No doubt due to Monroe's position as prime minister, Alderdice became government leader in the Council in 1928.

In a radio broadcast in February 1928, Monroe announced that he would not be a candidate in the upcoming general election.[49] MHAs fanned out to determine who might be interested in leading the Party. William J. Browne, John Puddester, and Tom Power became "a delegation on behalf of the Party" and went to see Alderdice. Either Alderdice was expecting to be asked, or he was quickly convinced: either way, he immediately agreed to take on the leadership and "make some return for what [he had] received since [he] came here."[50] In a way, Alderdice was a logical replacement for Monroe. His role as government leader in the Legislative Council had given him a taste for politics, and an understanding of the workings of the legislature.

Both St. John's papers praised Alderdice's ascension to the prime ministership on August 14. The *Daily News* editorialized that "it would be difficult to find one so well qualified" for the role, adding that Alderdice's "tactfulness and sincerity ... high ideals, strict honour and strong conviction [would be useful assets] to lead his country safely and surely along the paths of prosperity."[51] The *Telegram* showed less adulation, but commended the new prime minister for wasting "no time in selecting his colleagues [in Cabinet] ... it is an infusion of new blood."[52]

For the October 1928 election, the Conservatives rebranded themselves the UNP. The campaign was a bare-knuckle fight between Alderdice's UNP and a reunified Liberal-FPU Party under

---

49 O'Flaherty, *Lost Country*, 341–43.

50 Browne, *Eighty-four Years*, 160.

51 *Daily News*, August 17, 1928.

52 *Evening Telegram*, August 17, 1928.

Sir Richard Squires. Squires had been disgraced, forced from power in a Cabinet revolt after his second election win in 1923 amid accusations of bribing voters with public funds. The UNP made the most of Squires's past, and their election advertising depicted Squires, the FPU's William Coaker, and Peter Cashin as opportunistic cats, ready to pounce on a canary that represented the public Treasury: "Wouldn't they like to get their hands on it again. Will you allow those hungry office seekers to again raid the Public Treasury?" The only way to keep out the rapacious cats, according to the UNP, was to elect Alderdice "and stability."[53] Alderdice argued that a return to Squires was a return to corruption and inept government. The UNP charged that a Squires government would deter unnamed investors anxious to put their money into Newfoundland. Alderdice's election material claimed that "this budding international development would shrivel and wither if men, whose unsavoury record is known throughout the business world better than in their own country, should by any unfortunate move gain the reins of Government."[54]

The editorialists at both St. John's papers tried to sway public opinion by portraying the "unholy alliance between Squires and Cashin" as political opportunism. Cashin, a Liberal in Squires's 1923 government, united with other discontented Liberals who joined Conservatives to form a party under Monroe in time for the 1924 election. Monroe won the election, but Cashin quit two years later after new tariffs were added to goods including cigarettes, tobacco, rope, twines, fishing nets, butter, and margarine.[55]

---

53 UNP advertisement, *Daily News,* October 2, 1928.

54 UNP advertisement, *Daily News*, September 29, 1928.

55 Baker, "Newfoundland in the 1920s," in History 3120 Manual: Newfoundland History, 1815–1972, rev. ed. (Division of Continuing Studies, Memorial University of Newfoundland, St. John's, 1994).

He sat in the House with a group that eventually united with Squires and Coaker in 1928. "There is no evidence of friendship between the two," the *Daily News* wrote of Squires and Cashin on October 2, and although "Sir Richard's grandiloquent recital of the burying of the hatchet was very touching, [it] was not at all convincing." The two only associated at all, according to the paper, "through the efforts of Sir William Coaker." The papers kept up the attack against Squires in the days leading up to the October 29 vote. "Squires gets frantic S.O.S. from Corner Brook" ran the headline in the *Daily News* five days before polling day. The Liberal leader had apparently rushed off "by special train in [an] attempt to stem [a] landslide against him in [his] own district." Alderdice and his minister of Justice, W.J. Howley, were on their way to Corner Brook the next day after "excellent meetings" in Bay Roberts and Spaniard's Bay.

In retaliation, the Liberals made accusations against Alderdice, of running independent candidates in an attempt to siphon Opposition votes. The *Daily News* dismissed these accusations as a "silly lie."

On election day, Alderdice and the UNP were defeated, and Squires returned as prime minister. The Liberals won 19 seats, the FPU 9; those 28 seats more than doubled the 12 seats taken by Alderdice and the UNP. The two winning parties managed 54.5 per cent of the votes, while Alderdice polled 43.3 per cent. The eight independent candidates polled 2.2 per cent, and played the role of spoiler in three districts, two of which were won by the Conservatives. Neither of the St. John's papers commented at any length about the election results; they merely printed the returns and virtually ignored Squires's electoral comeback. On the day they would have been proclaiming an Alderdice victory, their main headlines were that the German airship *Graf Zeppelin* was passing over Newfoundland on the return leg of its first transatlantic voyage between Germany and Lakehurst, New Jersey.

Alderdice had spent 10 weeks as prime minister. Despite the loss, he was committed to staying on as party leader and holding Squires and the new government to account until the next election. It took hard work by Alderdice and the rest of the Opposition, and the intervention of the worldwide Great Depression, to give his party a fighting chance against Squires the next time Newfoundlanders voted. In the interim, he had to endure taunts from members in the new government, those whom Alderdice and his supporters had vilified during the campaign. Those years became a test of Alderdice's ability to take the tough knocks that politics delivers. In his reply to the Speech from the Throne on April 17, 1929, Alderdice chastised Squires for glossing over the unemployment problem during the election campaign. "We were told that as soon as the present Government got into power, the day of unemployment would be over," he told the House. "The land would be flowing with milk and honey." He concluded that the appointment of a Commission to study the unemployment problem was because Squires was "afraid to take on the responsibility."[56]

Squires did not miss the opportunity to put the former prime minister in his place: "Those who can look back upon more than twenty years in and out of this Chamber … realize the difficulty which a new-comer [Alderdice] has in getting into the swing of public affairs." He acknowledged Alderdice's time in the House's upper chamber, concluding that "as the years go on, day by day, he will be given a further training."[57] Days later, during the budget debate, Cashin needled Alderdice about government spending leading up to the October 1928 election. "The Alderdice party

---

56 *Proceedings*, April 17, 1929, 15.

57 Ibid., 17.

spent some hundreds of thousands of dollars during the last election," Cashin charged, "and now I am going to tell how they spent it." Alderdice protested, "We were not in power then." Cashin had the last word: "I agree that you were not in power then, but when I am finished, you will see what I mean."[58] Cashin recited a list of what he considered questionable expenses: "They even paid out of the Treasury of the country the man who nominated my opponent—paid him $30 for the job. Isn't that beautiful[?]"[59]

Alderdice's four years in the Opposition provide some insight into his views on the worsening economy, as well as his approach to emerging issues around workers' rights, including working conditions and pay for the loggers who supplied Newfoundland's two paper mills and the hundreds of clerks who worked for Water Street merchants. Alderdice also developed his views on the reimplementation of income tax and prohibition. He received the training Squires had taunted him about in his reply to the Speech from the Throne in 1928, after all.

Alderdice's party was essentially the same as the one that formed the ministry under Monroe. The politicians were generally businessmen and professionals regarded by their supporters at the *Daily News* as "men of integrity," in contrast to the "political adventurers" running under the Squires-Coaker banner.[60] Lawyer Edward Emerson, who squeaked in by 20 votes in Placentia East in 1928, acknowledged the conservative and business-class roots of the UNP when he appealed for help for fishermen in April 1931: "We on this side of the house are supposed to be the 'blue bloods.' We are supposed to be the merchants' party."[61]

---

58 Ibid., May 1, 1929, 120.

59 Ibid., 121.

60 *Daily News*, September 29, 1928; October 2, 1928.

61 *Proceedings*, April 21, 1931, 229.

Alderdice suggested that some of this labelling was political in-
nuendo, a deliberate attempt by Squires and his supporters to
cast the UNP as profit-driven businessmen who cared little for
the general welfare of the population. "I am not very rich although
I am spoken of as being such," he told the House during the
1929 debate on the reintroduction of income tax. "Several times
at public dinners and other places when the subject of income
taxation has been mentioned, everybody looked at me. I really
do not know which is the worse plight to be in, to be wealthy
and have the reputation of being poor, or of being poor and
having the reputation of being wealthy."[62]

Alderdice supported the reinstatement of income tax, which
had been removed by Monroe in 1925. "I am heartily in accord

Daily News building, Duckworth Street, St. John's, post-1892. *ASC, Coll-
137, 02.01.002*

---

62 Ibid., May 3, 1929, 163.

with the proposed income tax," he told the House on May 3, 1929. "I pay what is required to the utmost farthing and all Companies I am associated with have always paid to the last cent." Yet he regarded parts of the income tax Bill as being "too drastic," especially the tax rate, which was significantly higher than that in place in Canada. He also proposed a higher discount for those who paid their tax account in cash, a measure that, if adopted, "would be very helpful and the people would pay the tax with a greater willingness and feel they were not being fleeced."[63]

Alderdice worked hard to be progressive in his outlook. He spoke eloquently of the problems facing the fishery, noting that establishing strict standards for codfish being exported, and the regulation of those exports, would be instrumental in helping "absorb and solve the unemployment situation." Although he was a well-known and successful businessman, Alderdice was not involved in the fish export trade, and that may have allowed him to view the industry with some detachment. "I believe that the problem of price can be solved," he told the House in June 1930, "but when we meet men so temperamental, so full of idiosyncrasies as the fish buyers of Newfoundland, I am not surprised."[64] He accused merchants of competing heavily to buy high quantities of fish at high prices in 1929, only to turn around in the spring of 1930 and effectively dump the fish in the market with resulting low prices and the loss of $500,000 in value to Newfoundland: "If the merchant through bad selling, bad handling, loses money, say this fall, then they start the new season with a very pessimistic frame of mind." Alderdice concluded, "the pity of it is that this foolishness re-acts against the fisherman: he pays the price every time."[65]

---

63 Ibid.

64 Ibid., June 12, 1930, 145.

65 Ibid.

Alderdice was also willing to do battle with the foreign investors behind Newfoundland's pulp and paper industry. The Squires government had brought in reforms to change the way loggers were paid. The Bill was introduced by Kenneth McKenzie Brown, the MHA for Twillingate, who began his working life at the pulp and paper mill in Grand Falls and had become involved with the union. Brown recounted how the companies paid wages to the loggers until about 1921 and then, in response to changing economic times, reverted to a "sub-contract" system. This meant that the men were essentially hired as companies and became responsible for all their own expenses. Brown recounted a case in 1925 "where a party of seven men worked for six months and when … the accounts [were] fixed up, they found they were three or four dollars in debt."[66]

The loggers' reforms instigated by Squires were intended to legislate a minimum wage of 35 cents an hour and set the standard size of a cord of wood at 128 feet. Alderdice agreed to both counts, saying he had "heard in certain sections where a cord of wood was being based at 142 feet … This, I think is a gross injustice." He was most eloquent on the issue of loggers' pay: "When we take into consideration that these men are in the water practically all day, and the laborious and dangerous work they have to perform, I certainly do not think 35c. an hour is out of the way." He described the principle of the Bill as "a good one" and believed that "anything that would make the conditions better for the logging men should be introduced."[67]

But Alderdice did not always side with the workers. A Bill to regulate shop closing times in St. John's East and West was produced in response to a petition from 1,200 shop clerks in St. John's.

66 Ibid., May 13, 1931, 495.
67 Ibid., 496–97.

Squires introduced the Bill but it was overshadowed by the opposition of his own finance minister, Peter Cashin, who claimed shop closing times was an issue that should have been dealt with by the municipal council. Cashin argued that "the clerks of Water Street are being used by the merchants," who wanted to institute shop closing rules to disadvantage 14 of their downtown competitors, and put them out of business.[68]

It was true that shop clerks worked long hours. John Puddester, the Opposition member for Bay de Verde, spoke to the need "to protect at least 1,200 clerks … from going to work every day in the year from eight in the morning to ten at night." Alderdice joined the debate several times to ask questions, but he was most forceful when the suggestion was made that the abuse of clerks by shop owners could be controlled by implementing over-

Bowring Brothers, one of the many merchants on Water Street, St. John's, ca. 1920. *ASC, Coll-137, 02.01.020*

---

68 Ibid., 504.

time pay at time and a half: "I see no reason why we should enter into and try and destroy the confidence that exists between the employer and employee in St. John's today." He told the House that none of the clerks had mentioned wanting to receive overtime pay, concluding that "if they are willing, when it is necessary, to work without overtime, I say we should not interfere with the pleasant relations that exist today."[69]

Other clues to Alderdice's personality and political leanings were revealed in his legislative debates. During the 1928 campaign, it was suggested that Squires would move to restrict the availability of liquor once he took office. Alderdice's views on this issue could be regarded as self-serving, since it was generally believed he himself enjoyed a few drinks. Still, his public comments reveal something of a civil libertarian outlook. "Now, I am not a prohibitionist," he told the House in the debate on a Bill that would standardize the size of bottles, and, therefore, make it more difficult to smuggle alcohol. "I am at all times at the service of anyone who can think out a plan for the curtailment of alcoholic liquors in this country as long as it does not interfere with the exercise of man's freedom of action."[70]

In the same debate, Alderdice recounted a conversation he had had with the head of the controller's department during his time as prime minister in 1928: "It was a source of complaint amongst the supporters of the Monroe Party and my party ... that he [the controller] should give [purchase] orders only to the supporters of our respective administrations." In a meeting at the prime minister's office, Alderdice asked the controller: "Do you know what I expect you to do? I expect you to run your department

---

69 Ibid., 526.
70 Ibid., May 28, 1929, 506.

as you would run a business. Buy good liquor for the people, and give the country a square deal, and I do not care where you buy your liquor so long as it is of good quality and at a fair price."[71] Alderdice's last remark might well have been a jab at Squires, since it was widely felt in UNP circles that Canadian distilleries had financed a significant part of the 1928 Liberal campaign.

Alderdice's deepest interest in, and sharpest criticism of, the Squires government was on fiscal matters. He regarded Squires's Economic Commission, set up in the wake of the 1928 election, as nothing more than "a shock absorber," necessary to "soothe the disappointed electors" in the wake of Squires's election promise of improved employment opportunities. Alderdice argued that if the prime minister had been candid at the time the Commission was established, "he would admit ... he had not the faintest hope, he had not the faintest idea that they were going to be able to accomplish anything."[72] Newfoundland, in Alderdice's opinion, was "fortunate to have two or three industries ... capable of considerable expansion"—chief among them the fishery. Self-interest was evident in this statement as well, given that his business sold nets, twine, and other fishing gear to thousands of fishermen. His criticism focused on the low quality of Newfoundland fish, and he argued that the issue had to be addressed with tough and enforceable regulations. But he also felt that, if the industry were to have a future, higher prices would have to be paid to fishermen. It was, he stated, "our bounden duty to see that it is remunerative for the people who pursue it, and that it is made as congenial as possible." He decried the migration from fishing communities, the lack of "mention of the fishery in the [school] curriculum," and the lack

---

71 Ibid., 507.
72 Ibid., June 12, 1930, 143.

of modern amenities, such as moving pictures and travelling libraries, in small towns. "The cream of the country are leaving us; the young men from 20 and the young women are leaving this country and the worst of it is that they are the best of them," he argued. "Life must be made more livable for the outport people in the fishing business."[73]

As Opposition leader, and as a member of the Legislative Council, Alderdice was supportive of government regulation of industries and activities that were "a factor in the industrial life" of Newfoundland. He supported a Bill in the spring of 1928 that set rules for the gathering and export of wild fruit and berries. "It was proper that every safeguard should be taken to see that the consumer received a good article," he told his upper House colleagues, "to see that they are properly packed and that the quality is up to standard."[74] Where matters of health were involved, as in the Bill regulating the practice of optometry, Alderdice again had a common sense contribution to the debate: "This bill will be the means of preventing the tampering of eyes by unskilled and unlicensed persons."[75] He eschewed the manner in which the civil service was being run, called for competitive exams to be introduced, and wanted "to see our civil service work a little harder and [be] paid a little more."[76]

Alderdice rejected special treatment for the wealthy and, despite his business background, sounded somewhat like a populist. This was demonstrated in his first year as Opposition leader, when the contentious matter of penalizing drunk driving arose during

---

73 Ibid., 145.

74 Proceedings, Legislative Council Proceedings, June 5, 1928, 50.

75 Ibid., May 29, 1928.

76 Ibid., May 22, 1928.

debate of a Bill to regulate traffic on Newfoundland's still sparse highways. The Squires government proposed a fine of "$10 or $20" for first-time offenders if they caused damage less than $25; and a fine of up to $250 for a second offence. "Well now, a wealthy man does not mind that," Alderdice protested, but declared that such a fine "would be a distinct hardship to a poor man ... This looks to me distinctly like class legislation." Intoxicated drivers should have few options once they were stopped by police. "I am of the opinion that the penalty [for] a person in the state of intoxication is not sufficiently severe," he said. "I think that the offender should not be allowed the option of a fine for the first and second offence."[77] He was similarly tough about the control of alcohol, especially in St. John's, where "if people can believe half of what they are told, we have some questionable dives in our midst." Those "dives" were selling liquor without a licence, and not necessarily liquor imported from regulated distilleries in Canada, the US, or the Caribbean. "It is to these houses that unsuspecting girls and men are induced by the apparent respectability of these houses ... and from there they often take their first downward step." He called for a Board of Liquor Control. "It may mean employment of extra officials," he said, "but I think that all of this is offset by the fact that it is assisting the police department in obtaining clues and evidence against shebeening."[78]

---

77 *Proceedings*, April 26, 1929, 56.

78 Ibid., May 28, 1929. The term *shebeening* originated in Ireland to describe the practice of selling illegally produced or illegally imported alcohol in an unlicensed establishment.

CHAPTER 4

Alderdice Comes to Power

Newfoundland has determined that it is time to change.
—*Daily News*, May 11, 1932

That political affairs are becoming more and more complicated goes without saying, so much so that people are in a maze.
—*Twillingate Sun*, April 23, 1932

Newfoundland society hobbled along into 1932. Squires was well into the fourth year of his term, and an election could not be far off. The next government would have to find a way out of the financial and economic mess the country was in or priva-tion and austerity would worsen. In early February 1932, the political landscape was further shaken with sensational charges from Squires's finance minister.

Cashin resigned from Cabinet on February 1, 1932, without explanation. Anticipation built in St. John's for the opening of the winter session of the House three days later. The economic crisis in Newfoundland and the government's worsening fiscal situa-tion were enough for the Squires ministry to battle; it did not need political scandal as well.[79] But that was what it got. When Cashin spoke on February 4, he levelled a barrage of charges at Squires and his government. He accused Squires of taking a $5,000 annual payment from the War Reparations Committee; the member for St. Barbe of forging another man's name in order to get a cheque from the fisheries department; and Cabinet minister Campbell of evading the payment of income tax[80] and of having been paid as immigration officer "in a country with no immigration."[81] Cashin also accused Squires of falsifying Cabinet minutes "in order to deceive the governor and some of his cabinet by covering up certain fees he had paid himself out of public funds."[82] He drew particular attention to payments from the German Reparations Fund to the German Reparations Commissioner, a position to which Squires was appointed on August 22, 1929:

> Those who fought for their country, and the relatives of those who died will, no doubt, feel aggrieved that no mean portion of their small material recompense falls into the hands of slackers, under the pitiful guise for services rendered. In view of the statements which I have made, which are, so help me God, to the best of my knowledge true, one is forced to the dreadful conclusion that what we won by honour and in death is falling to dishonour and decay ... Our comrades died for Newfoundland. If we break faith, they may not sleep.[83]

---

79 Noel, *Politics in Newfoundland*, 197.

80 Ibid.

81 Ibid., 201.

82 Ibid., 197–98.

83 *Proceedings*, February 16, 1932.

Thousands in St. John's were unemployed during the winter of 1932, and Cashin's accusations that the prime minister had been helping himself to public funds while the unemployed were forced to rely on six cents a day in dole payments "proved sensational and inflammatory."[84] A week later, hundreds marched to Squires's office at the courthouse and demanded higher benefits. They stood outside for hours, waiting for a meeting between their leaders and the prime minister. The meeting did not happen, so the mob forced its way inside and burst into Squires's office. "Squires was roughly jostled by the crowd," and calm was only restored when dole orders were distributed.[85]

The Opposition demanded that Cashin's charges be investigated by a Select Committee of MHAs. Squires amended that motion and got the House to agree that Middleton investigate whether he had been "deceived or induced by such deception to sign the Minutes in question."[86] The governor reported that the House did not have the constitutional authority to question the accuracy of the Minutes, but also concluded that the Minutes had not been falsified and he had not been deceived into signing them.[87] His report did not erase the accusations, since "there were unexplained discrepancies between [the Minutes in question] and the decisions recorded on the cabinet agenda from which the minutes were compiled [and] enough previously unknown facts had emerged to undermine any confidence that may have remained in the government."[88]

Squires had merely delayed a showdown. On March 23, he

---

84 Baker, "The Second Squires Administration and the Loss of Responsible Government, 1928–1934," 1994, http://www.ucs.mun.ca/~melbaker/1920s.htm.

85 Noel, *Politics in Newfoundland*, 198; *Evening Telegram*, February 12, 1932.

86 *Proceedings*, February 23, 1932, 24–25.

87 Ibid., Reply of His Excellency the Governor, March 22, 1932.

88 Noel, *Politics in Newfoundland*, 201.

provoked more public outrage when his government announced increases in customs duties and cuts in war veterans' pensions. These measures were recommended by Sir Percy Thompson, deputy chair of the UK Inland Revenue Board, who had been assigned to Newfoundland to fulfill one of the conditions of a $2 million loan advanced by four Canadian banks in the early summer of 1931.[89] The political cost to Squires was immediate: Harry Mosdell, a minister without portfolio, resigned, as did two government MHAs,[90] citing pension cuts and increased customs duties on foods such as flour, beef, and pork.

St. John's residents had seen and heard enough. A public meeting held at the LSPU Hall on April 4 brought demands that the charges against Squires and others be investigated. A committee formed at that meeting and, the next day, accompanied by thousands of city residents, the committee converged on the seat of government at Colonial Building to deliver their petition "protesting, in the name of justice and morality" the actions of the government.[91] They appeared at the entrance to the House of Assembly, and presented the petition to the Clerk, who read it into the record. After some procedural arguing about how to respond, a ruckus erupted in the gallery and outside the building. Rocks were thrown, windows smashed, and a crowd broke into the basement. They set fires, destroyed furniture, and looted offices and records. Squires tried to escape from the mob with a police escort through a side door, but the crowd saw him and closed in.

---

89 Ibid., 196–201.

90 Mosdell was MHA for Fortune Bay. The other two MHAs who resigned from the government to sit as Independents were John Parsons of Bay Roberts and Philip Fudge of Hermitage.

91 "Citizens' Meeting" (from *Daily News*, April 5, 1932), Newfoundland and Labrador Heritage, http://www.heritage.nf.ca/law/meetings_apr04.html.

A group of people, including some clergy, intervened. One of the protesters hit Squires in the face, but his rescuers eventually got him to safety in a home on Colonial Street. Later, he escaped from the city by automobile and went into hiding.[92]

Squires could no longer manoeuvre his way out of trouble. The political machinations of the legislature had been overtaken by strong public sentiment. Several thousand citizens were deputized to help keep the peace, and for good measure, the British cruiser HMS *Dragon* and its 400 crew arrived in St. John's on April 12. A day later, with Squires still in hiding, the government caucus met, and decided a general election should be held as soon as possible.[93]

The *Fishermen's Advocate* felt that the St. John's troubles were set up by the Opposition and supported by the Water Street merchants. Reporting on the riot at Squires's office at the Supreme Court, the paper wrote, "the intention of [Squires's] captors was to drown him in the harbour." It said the rioters "were mostly young men who [had] been prominent in all recent Opposition parades and meetings attacking the Government." As for the large crowds at the Colonial Building riot, the *Advocate* suggested, "the larger Water Street stores were closed during the parade. This was done to swell the number."[94]

Alderdice and his key people in the UNP were concerned about accusations that they played any role in the St. John's disturbances. Alderdice, along with John Puddester and Edward Emerson, signed a letter published in the *Twillingate Sun*, proclaiming that the event "included the best elements of [the] City, including

---

92 Noel, *Politics in Newfoundland*, 202.

93 Ibid.

94 *Advocate*, April 8, 1932.

clergy from all denominations," and that the trouble was caused by a group of young men and boys: "Any other description of events [is] entirely false, and meant solely to deceive Outport people."[95]

The demonstrations in St. John's were evidence of the desperate times confronting Newfoundland. It would not be easy to find a way out, since Newfoundland's principal industries—the cod and seal fisheries, iron ore mining, and newsprint production—were all geared toward export markets. Demand for those commodities was down, and prices had taken a serious tumble. The 1932 seal fishery was poor, the third lowest catch in half a century, according to the *Daily News*. Newfoundland sealers braved the dangers of the icefields at the Front to bring home 48,613 pelts that year, compared to 80,377 the previous year.

People hoped for a good cod fishery, although no one expected a miracle. The catch for 1931 was down for the fifth consecutive year, and the price was 30 per cent lower than it had been the year before. The Newfoundland cod that was shipped to Europe, dogged by its reputation for poor quality, fetched a lower price than cod from the island's main competitors in Norway and Iceland.

The legislative session ended on the last day of April, more than three weeks after the Colonial Building riot. That night, the UNP honoured Alderdice, who, a few days later, would lead them into the election.

Squires waited more than a week after the House closed to issue the writ for a June 11 election. In the Gazette Extraordinary, he also announced patronage appointments for three MHAs. The *Telegram* decried the appointments, referring to "the audacity of the government," and accused Squires of "exceed[ing] all bounds

---

95 F.C. Alderdice, letter to the editor, *Twillingate Sun*, April 16, 1932.

of decency and propriety." The outraged editor proclaimed "from first to last, it [the Squires government] has flouted public opinion and public interests. Now comes the time however, when public opinion will have its turn." There was no question of the paper's judgment of Squires and his government: "Out with them, and let them for a change earn a living by the sweat of their brow."[96]

The *Daily News* also attacked Squires, accusing him of leaving the calling of the election to "the very limit of procrastination possible under the Act." It concluded that Squires's long wait to call the vote signified "the unwillingness of the leader of the Government to face the electorate ... Newfoundland has determined that it is time for change." In an editorial on May 11, more vitriol was hurled at Squires for "putting off the evil day till the last minute—evil for him it will surely be."[97]

The *Evening Telegram* and the *Daily News* had aligned against Squires since his corruption troubles in the 1920s and unabashedly supported Alderdice during the election. They made no pretence of objectively reporting the campaign. The *Telegram* reported in rabid partisan detail on the Alderdice campaign in St. John's and used correspondents to provide details of major events in the outport campaigns. Most, if not all, of the *Telegram*'s correspondents were committee members of the UNP candidates in the districts. The *Daily News*, appearing to rely less on out-of-town correspondents, delivered a more straightforward, if still biased, account of events.

Half a dozen newspapers existed in Newfoundland during the early 1930s, and several papers based outside of St. John's also reported extensively on the campaign. In the lead-up to the election, the *Twillingate Sun*, which had supported Squires in 1928, was

---

96 *Evening Telegram*, May 11, 1932.
97 *Daily News*, May 11, 1932.

prepared to do so again in the spring of 1932, proclaiming that, while "the Country's affairs are in the process of a thorough over-hauling, it will be our duty to defend … the Government … as long as they are seeking out the remedies to rectify what has been the ills of the body politic …"[98] As the election got under way, the *Sun* declared it would be neutral, and accurately predicted the election in the district would be a close one. It also sounded a note of cynicism: "Many of the electorate in this vicinity think that changing the men is not going to be any more beneficial than for many years."[99]

The *Advocate*, the organ of the FPU, did not have the same clarity of vision. The FPU won nine seats in the 1928 election and helped bring Squires back to power through a coalition with the Liberals. The union paper felt that Squires was being treated poorly by "the Opposition press of St. John's [and while] it was very easy for the members of the Opposition and editors of the Tory papers to keep on circulating the base falsehoods [against the Squires government] it is not, however, easy for the Prime Minister or his Ministers to refute every hour these charges. This is beneath their dignity."[100] The *Advocate* did not actively support Squires and the Liberals, and was not overtly critical of Alderdice. It did foreshadow the loss of responsible government in 1934, when it reminded its readers to "place the very best interests of the country first, for this likely will be the last election fought as a Dominion."[101] The *Advocate* responded to accusations from "a writer of the city papers" that the *Advocate* was showing "benevolent

---

98 Ibid., April 16, 1932.
99 Ibid., April 23, 1932.
100 *Advocate*, March 26, 1932.
101 Ibid., May 20, 1932.

neutrality toward the Government" by replying "we have tried to be fair."[102] The paper was also clear, however, that should the campaign become partisan, it would come to the rescue of Squires and the Liberals. It said that the northern bays were "Liberal in politics and while many … are indifferent as regards Sir Richard Squires' return, yet the least said about him by the Opposition, the better." The editorial on May 20 concluded with this threat— "a very little of flimsy talk from the platform [criticizing Squires and the Liberals] would set the whole North alive and send Opposition candidates to Kingdom Come."

The Bay Roberts *Guardian* was as unabashed in its support of Squires and the Liberals as the St. John's papers were in their support of Alderdice. "Is Squires to be blamed for this?" the *Guardian* asked a week before the vote in its June 3 editorial titled "The Depression in Newfoundland." It posed another question: "Will the Alderdice-Monroe supporters dare tell us that Mr. Alderdice could have prevented the Depression from striking us, or if he had sufficient brains or desire and ability to conquer it when it did arrive?" This paper did not address the strong taint of scandal that followed Squires, but attempted to smear Alderdice, without offering any evidence of its insinuation: "We wonder how many lawyers and other candidates of the Alderdice Party, including Mr. Alderdice himself, is interested in large tracts of timber limits on the Labrador and elsewhere?" The paper implied, without invoking Squires's name, that Alderdice would be just as likely to bestow patronage as the Liberal leader—"we learned that Mr. Alderdice has promised all his 1928 defeated candidates a job if he is elected."[103]

On May 2, 1932, Coaker announced his retirement from

---

102 Ibid.
103 *Guardian*, May 3, 1932.

politics, citing "physical disabilities." In doing so, Coaker also effectively broke with Squires. Coaker had made his concerns about the state of elected government in Newfoundland known as far back as the FPU Annual Convention in November 1925, when he also first mentioned the value of government by commission.[104] During the 1932 campaign, he praised Alderdice for announcing "his intention of meeting [his] proposal of seven years ago, which was that a Commission should be established to govern the country."[105] In a line that could be taken as a tacit endorsement of Alderdice, Coaker added that if his ill health had not forced him to resign, he "would be actively associated with a policy advocated by [him] several years ago [government by commission]."[106]

Alderdice and the UNP promised to study the concept of government by commission if they won the election. Alderdice stated in the UNP manifesto, its election pamphlet, that "one of my first acts will be the appointment of a committee … to enquire into the desirability and feasibility to place the Country under a form of Commission of Government for a period of years." It concluded that if an investigation found the commission to be the

---

104 William F. Coaker, *Twenty Years of the Fishermen's Protective Union from 1909–1929* (1930; repr., St. John's, NL: Creative Printers, 1984), 235–36. Coaker advocated an elected commission of nine people that would have a 10-year term of office. He proposed three members from Catholic districts, and three each from the West Coast and Conception Bay. These nine members would elect a chairman, who would become prime minister. Coaker suggested all legislation be published so that the public could discuss it before the politicians passed it into law. He believed that the reforms would "procure retrenchment and place the fishing industry on a sound businesslike basis." Coaker proposed that such a system would also "cut out graft, reduce the Civil Service list to its proper proportion, dispense, for a period, with the animosities and bitterness of party strife and permit the country to concentrate upon vital matters …"

105 *Advocate*, May 6, 1932.

106 Ibid., May 2, 1932.

The cover of Alderdice's *Manifesto* for the 1932 election. In it, he outlines New-foundland's financial problems and his party's proposed solutions, notably his intention to investigate the possibility of government by commission. *Centre for Newfoundland and Labrador Studies, Queen Elizabeth II Library, Memorial University of Newfoundland*

favoured option, Alderdice would hold a referendum, promising "no action will be taken that does not first have the consent of the people."[107] The *Advocate* was skeptical about Alderdice's commitment. "What is strange about the pledge of the Opposition leader," a May 27 editorial announced, "is that so few of his candidates have referred to the matter from the public platform." People in the northern districts were requested to "ask the candidate at a public meeting to declare his position ... and if he is not able to come out square-footed for such a proposition, tell him straight that you cannot vote for him." With or without such a debate, the *Advocate* was convinced that worse days lay ahead for Newfoundland. "The Country is within two years of the greatest crisis of its history," the May 27 editorial concluded. "Confederation, or default on the interest on the bonds, or Government by Commission, will have to come during the next year or two."

The St. John's papers generally ignored the warnings from the *Advocate* and focused instead on the UNP platform. On May 28, the *Evening Telegram* quoted from a speech in which Alderdice promised to reduce the level of taxation: "I am convinced it will be possible," he said, "that taxation should, and can, be reduced." He did not explain how that would happen, given the devastating cycle of deficit spending and borrowing that had gone on for many years, but the promise was repeated in the party's manifesto.[108] Alderdice also committed himself to "devising means" to restore education funding and to make changes to the school curriculum that would align it with the "life, thought and industry of the country ... [to prepare people for jobs] in the fisheries, mining

---

107 *Manifesto of Hon. F.C. Alderdice, Leader of the United Newfoundland Party, 1932* (UNP, May 1932), 13–14.

108 Ibid., 6.

industry, business or the professions."[109] The paper explained its support for Alderdice and the UNP: "The community as a whole has reason to share his views, [which lie] in efficiency of administration, the lightening of the burden of taxation, and the increasing of the earning power of the people ... because it is convinced that Mr. Alderdice and his party are earnest in their desire to effect these necessary reforms, this paper gives the whole of its support to the campaign."[110]

Leading up to the election call, and through the campaign itself, Squires was besieged with requests for private donations of money, demands for fishing gear and engines, and appeals for government jobs in exchange for offers of support. One man wrote to ask for "a loan of one hundred and fifty dollars to get a fit-out for the fishery."[111] A woman from Tilton East told him about a "terrible headache" and her need of a donation to get to the hospital at St. Anthony. She wrote a second letter that day asking Squires for a "pair of second-hand [glasses he didn't] use [as her] eyes [were] terrible bad. [She was] almost blind."[112] Some letters made a direct link between a promise fulfilled and a vote for Squires. A St. John's man asked, "I wonder if you are going to place me in a job this coming election," adding that "with myself and wife, two votes will be given to the man who will give me a helping hand."[113] Another asked if Squires would back a $200 note at the bank for three months: "as you know, I worked hard for

---

109 Ibid., 12.

110 *Evening Telegram*, May 28, 1932.

111 Archives and Special Collections, Queen Elizabeth II Library, Memorial University of Newfoundland (ASC), Coll-250, 2.28.005, Letter to Squires from Boyd's Cove, May 27, 1932.

112 Ibid., Letter from Tilton East, May 2, 1932.

113 Ibid., Letter to Squires, May 3, 1932.

your party in the last general election, and in the bye-election."[114] A Glovertown lumber contractor intimated that a few bottles of liquor would help him entice some Alderdice supporters to vote for Squires: "I want you to send me in a private box a few bottles of good boose, mosly rum. This will be confidential, you need not worry."[115]

Squires wrote personal replies to those who asked for donations. "I am unable to assist you by way of a loan," he wrote the St. John's man who asked for an engine to outfit his fishing boat, "because, to be quite frank with you, I have not the money to lend."[116] He told another man, "I have been identified for some years with one of the largest Outport supply firms in the country [and because of the] disastrous results of the past couple of years ... I now find myself in the position where I have to approach the Banks for accommodation to carry on during the coming season ..."[117]

In late March 1932, Squires, in an effort to bring spending in line with declining revenue, and to ensure that the government did not default, introduced more austerity measures. He brought in a "temporary surtax" on customs and excise duties and import taxes, increasing the duty by 3 per cent on numerous items and extending it to previously untaxed items such as flour, fishery salt, and gasoline. The government also reduced the pensions paid to war veterans.

Under the banner "Let Alderdice Give Newfoundland a Chance," the *Daily News* predicted that the excesses of the Squires government, and decisions in "its expiring moments" to give pen-

---

114 Ibid., Letter to Squires, May 2, 1932.

115 Ibid., Letter to Squires, June 3, 1932.

116 Ibid., Squires [letter] to a St. John's man, May 7, 1932.

117 Ibid.

sions and government jobs to retiring politicians, would not go over well: "The public who has had to face increased postages, increased taxes, and reduced public services ... will derive slight comfort ..."[118]

While the election became an outlet for people's pent-up frustration, it also kindled hope that, with the right kind of leadership, Newfoundland might find its way to surer financial footing. In the opening campaign meeting for the UNP at the Star Hall in St. John's on May 8, Alderdice capitalized on the accusations against Squires and other members of the government who had "enriched themselves" at the expenses of the treasury. He also made a direct appeal to women, who had obtained the right to vote in 1925, promising that "women of the whole island would benefit, for the first matter to be taken up would be to arrange for profitable avenues of employment."[119]

In his "pledge," intended to set the tone for the kind of government he would run—and distinguish it from that of Squires—Alderdice laid out three principles of the UNP campaign. First, UNP candidates were "coming forward in this crisis to bring the country back to prosperity, without hope for reward"; second, the merit principle would be paramount in appointment to government jobs, that "not a single person would be appointed over the heads of those already in the service"; and third, recent appointments by Squires "would be removed."[120]

Alderdice switched districts for the 1932 election, giving up St. John's East for St. John's West, both two-member constituencies. On the night he announced the decision, he returned to another key part of his campaign platform: solving the unem-

---

118 *Daily News*, May 9, 1932.

119 *Evening Telegram*, May 14, 1932.

120 *Daily News*, May 9, 1932.

Richard and Helena Squires on official tour in Naples, 1921, during Squires's first term as Newfoundland's prime minister. *The Rooms Provincial Archives of Newfoundland and Labrador, VA 157-89*

ployment problem. The *Evening Telegram* reported: "[Alderdice] believed that in three months after the election all the factories would be working at full staff at least three-quarters full time."[121]

It is questionable whether Alderdice actually believed such a rapid transformation could take place in the Newfoundland economy. Indeed, he publicly recognized Newfoundland's dire financial straits, noting that, in the years ahead, "it would be necessary ... to go to the banks and financial interests for assistance."[122] Certainly, no optimism was felt in the northern outports, where the FPU power base resided. The *Advocate*, laying out its views in an editorial on May 20 titled "The Question at Issue," concluded that "no change of government will help the country out of its present dis-

---

121 *Evening Telegram*, May 17, 1932.
122 Ibid.

tress," and that, furthermore, "the winter of 1933 will find the people just as badly off as last winter." The article targeted the quality of the people standing for election in 1932 who "[were] appealing to the electorate as if though they [were] preparing for a Garden Party." In its final indictment of the quality of the candidates offering for election in 1932, the paper concluded that "not five realize the serious situation that will confront the successful party."

In the days after the election call, St. John's was abuzz with news of candidates leaving for their districts and with the intrigue of who would have the courage to put their names forward to run with Squires. Joseph Burke, a St. John's butcher rumoured to be a Squires candidate for St. John's East, "was approached by the Prime Minister," the *Telegram* reported on May 16, but turned him down. This was perceived as an honourable rejection of Squires, noting the "well-known butcher … refused Government orders to supply two big institutions," intimating that Burke refused to be bought off by such a corrupt regime. More than a week after the start of the campaign, the *Telegram* said that Squires was short nine candidates, and it reported that he had left his seat in Corner Brook to run in Trinity South "where Mr. Harold Mitchell's election seems certain."

The *Telegram* heaped vitriol on Cabinet minister Dr. Alex Campbell, whom Cashin had earlier accused of evading income tax: "Dr. Campbell is having a hard time telling the people in St. George's why he turned down the delegation which came to St. John's last year to protest against the flooding of the country with P.E.I. produce whilst the local product was allowed to rot." It also claimed to have seen a letter from Campbell to a personal friend, in which he confided "meeting with a great deal of opposition in his tour of the district."[123]

---

123 *Evening Telegram*, May 16, 1932.

Squires's wife, Lady Helena Squires, ran in the district of Twillingate. The Opposition and the St. John's papers portrayed her as an isolated candidate with little in the way of local support. In dispatches from their correspondent, the *Telegram* reported that Lady Squires "arrived [in Twillingate] on Friday to the coolest reception imaginable accorded her—not a solitary individual to greet her and no one to escort her to the hotel or even carry her luggage."[124] Meanwhile, UNP candidate Norman Gray had arrived the previous day "and was accorded the biggest reception ever given to a candidate in recent years," including a motorboat escort via Shoal Tickle where he was welcomed "with volleys of musketry by voters."[125]

The controversy even followed a politician who had decided not to run in 1932. Former MHA Richard Hibbs had been rewarded by a Squires patronage appointment. On the evening of May 12, he faced an unruly mob outside the front door of his farm in Kelligrews. The *Telegram* referred to the incident as a "commotion" and said people gathered to show "their resentment to Mr. Hibbs because of the work done by the Highroads [in the area and] the using of Highroads machinery on Mr. Hibbs' farm." Hibbs holed up inside his home as the protesters shouted at him to remove the machinery, or "they would not be responsible for the consequence ..." At some point during the confusion, he dashed to his car, and escaped. The paper reported that news of the tense situation was relayed to the two Liberal candidates campaigning in nearby Topsail, who "did not proceed further but retired to the City where they later heard the particulars from Mr. Hibbs."[126]

While the St. John's papers found fault with all aspects of the

---

124 Ibid., May 17, 1932.

125 Ibid.

126 Ibid., May 13, 1932.

Squires campaign, there was no such issue with the "heroes" leaving St. John's to campaign for Alderdice in the outports. The
Telegram reported on nearly all the UNP candidates as they left
for their districts. "Harold Earle left for Fogo where he has the
assurance of a large majority," it reported on May 13, and noted
also that Captain William Winsor left by SS *Home* for Bonavista
North—"indicators point to an easy victory for captain 'Billy,'
whose opponent is not yet selected." Hebert Quinton travelled by
train for Bonavista South where "repeated demands were made
for Mr. Quinton to come out on the platform ... Cheers were also
given for Mr. Alderdice." William Walsh left by train for Placentia
West, where he planned to campaign by motorboat. J.C. Puddester
drove to Carbonear to begin his campaign.[127]

The same campaign event was rarely reported on by multiple
papers. One exception, however, was Squires's tour through the
northern part of Conception Bay several days before the vote. The
Bay Roberts *Guardian*, which earlier in the campaign concluded
that voters "have almost lapsed into a state of indifference and
hopelessness," regarded Squires's late campaign rally in Clarke's
Beach a rousing success: "Fully 1,000 persons [attended and
Squires] was listened to with rapt attention." He started speaking
at 4 p.m. from a platform near the railway station, and engaged
the audience for two hours. The *Guardian* concluded that "Clarke's
Beach is 90% Squires."[128]

The *Telegram*'s coverage of the late push by Squires reached a
different conclusion. "The same cold reception was accorded him"
everywhere he went, according to "reliable reports" gathered by
the paper. There were "jeers" at Upper Island Cove, and while "the

127 Ibid.
128 *Guardian*, June 10, 1932.

Prime Minister did his best to put some enthusiasm into the meeting" in Long Pond, Conception Bay, he "utterly failed." The reception was just as hostile at a meeting in nearby Middle Bight, where the audience cheered for Alderdice once Squires began to speak. "Sir Richard was on his feet for 10 minutes," according to the paper's account, "but didn't speak for longer than two. The people simply wouldn't listen to him."[129]

Although most media coverage focused on the personalities of the politicians, both the *Daily News* and the *Advocate* reported on the "proposal" for a third paper mill to be built on the Gander River. The UNP insisted that the third mill was a bona fide proposal that Squires and his government had mishandled. Alderdice had spoken on the matter several times, promising in the party's manifesto "to spare no effort to make it an accomplished fact." On May 26, the *Daily News* published an anonymous article under the headline "Proof That Squires Wrecked the Gander," which claimed that the Reids "submitted a very tangible proposition ... but that it was impossible to get for it even reasonable consideration."

The *Advocate* refuted the allegation and printed an article under the headline "Another Matter Misunderstood—The Gander Proposition." It stated that it was "authorized by Sir William Coaker [to] state that no concrete proposition ... that would be acceptable to Newfoundland was ever submitted to the Executive ... had such a proposition been submitted to the executive it would have been accepted or the Squires administration would have gone to pieces."[130]

But Squires himself was the issue that dominated the election campaign; he had become a symbol of all that was wrong with

---

129 *Evening Telegram*, June 10, 1932.
130 *Advocate*, May 20, 1932.

Newfoundland politics. The St. John's papers and the UNP concluded that petty and personal priorities were put ahead of the
common good. The poor economic times that confronted Newfoundland at the onset of the Great Depression were made even
more difficult because of financial decisions that had been made
decades before. The colony had spent tens of millions on the railway to spur economic development. The decision to raise and
fund the Royal Newfoundland Regiment was costly both financially and in the loss of human life. Successive governments ran
deficits in relatively good times and covered the shortfall with
borrowed money rather than owning up to the problems by
cutting services or raising taxes. As Sidney Noel writes, "since no
administration after that of Sir Robert Bond had made provision
for a sinking fund, the only way in which matured loans could be
redeemed was by additional borrowing."[131]

The *Daily News* focused on "the vital necessity for change,"
casting the Alderdice team as a group of right-minded patriots
doing their duty for the country, and pointed to "the number of
independent men who have enrolled under his banner ... and
seek nothing from the treasury."[132] The implication, of course, was
that the Squires-led Liberals were out to make personal gains, and
that the "independent men" under Alderdice's banner could well
afford to live off their own efforts as lawyers, businessmen, and
other self-employed occupations.

The *Telegram* asked people to tune to radio station VONA on
the night of June 10 for "the final shot of the campaign" from Alderdice. "We are going to be elected," Alderdice proclaimed during

---

131 Noel, *Politics in Newfoundland*, 188. Bond was in power from 1900 to
1909.

132 *Daily News*, May 9, 1932.

his speech. He dismissed suggestions that Newfoundland might default ("I hesitate to think for this moment that this [default] might be possible, much less likely") or that the country was near bankruptcy ("[N]othing of the sort. After all, have we not assets in the form of natural resources to fully cover our borrowings?").[133]

It took several days for final election counts, but it was evident early on that Alderdice and the UNP would have a massive victory. On Monday, June 13, two days after the voting ended, the *Telegram* reported that Alderdice's UNP was leading everywhere except Humber. The biggest storyline was that businessman and World War I veteran Harold Mitchell had defeated Squires in Trinity South by 679 votes. It was deemed a "landslide."

According to the *Telegram*, Alderdice's district of St. John's West was the first to report. It was one of three double-member constituencies in 1932; the other two were St. John's East and Harbour Main-Bell Island. Alderdice and his running mate, Patrick F. Halley, polled nearly three times as many votes as the Liberal candidates, and finished with 72.4 per cent support. The margin for the UNP was even higher in St. John's West, with Alderdice's party taking 83.6 per cent of the vote. Ferryland had the distinction of providing the biggest margin of victory—UNP candidate Michael J. Shea won with 85.9 per cent of the vote.

Only two members of Squires's Liberals survived the rout: Gordon Bradley in Humber and Richard Starkes in Green Bay, with 54 per cent and 54.1 per cent of the vote, respectively. Lady Squires performed much better in Twillingate than the *Telegram* had predicted, coming within 273 votes of Norman Gray, and taking 42 per cent of the vote, the highest percentage of any of the losing Liberal candidates, and half a point higher than her husband

---

133 *Evening Telegram*, June 11, 1932.

in Trinity South. The *Telegram* reported that Lady Squires had been defeated "despite her every artifice," a comment on which the paper did not elaborate. The *Advocate* admitted the magnitude of Alderdice's victory: "We must confess … that the victory of the Opposition has been more sweeping than we thought would be the case … it seems apparent that St. John's and Conception Bay voted heavily, as did also Ferryland."[134] It implied there was not much interest in the election in the North, where voting was "light."

Mitchell's win was celebrated in St. John's,[135] where he was given a hero's welcome when he returned from his successful campaign against Squires in Trinity South. "The Return of the Victor," the *Telegram* headlined its coverage, noting *"The Telegram* finds it difficult adequately to congratulate Mr. Mitchell on his accomplishment." Mitchell—"the vanquisher of Sir Richard Squires"—arrived in St. John's the evening of June 14, with about 250 supporters from Trinity South. He was cheered as he travelled through Harbour Grace, Bay de Verde, Port de Grave, and Harbour Main districts. In Spaniard's Bay, "the procession was halted when a band played several lively airs and farewelled them out of the settlement." At Cross Roads near Paradise, Mitchell left his automobile and sat in a wagon that was pulled along by ropes held by ex-servicemen. Lieutenant H.B. Herder read an effusive statement on behalf of war

134 *Advocate*, June 17, 1932.

135 Mitchell, a successful businessman who had taken over his father's brokerage firm, was also a war hero, having made sergeant with the Royal Newfoundland Regiment at Suvla Bay in late September 1915. At that time, the Battle for the Dardanelles had been all but lost. The British were providing less than one-third of the requested ground-troop reinforcements, and all that was left was to wait for the official order to evacuate the Gallipoli Peninsula. That order was given in December, the same month that Mitchell contracted typhoid fever. He was discharged as medically unfit in April 1917. Once home in Newfoundland, he turned his attention to assisting veterans and became founder and first president of the Great War Veterans Association (GWVA).

veterans: "Your former comrades-in-arms. You won the greatest contest in the history of Newfoundland." The Methodist Guards led the parade into St. John's as people sang "Happy Days Are Here Again." Bunting was displayed along the route to Alderdice's house on Park Place, where Mitchell was given another ovation, as "the honoured chieftain, Mr. Alderdice, spoke from an open window." The festivities at Park Place concluded with a band playing a verse from "The Ode to Newfoundland."[136] The parade then wound its way to Mitchell's home, where he concluded his speech with a prophetic recitation of lines from Kipling's poem "Recessional." Kipling had written it at the time of Queen Victoria's Diamond Jubilee, when the British Empire was at its peak, and two destructive world wars were yet to be fought. Its words could well portend the trouble that lay ahead for Newfoundland:

> The tumult and the shouting dies;
> The Captains and the Kings depart:
> Still stands Thine ancient sacrifice,
> An humble and a contrite heart.
> Lord God of Hosts, be with us yet,
> Lest we forget—lest we forget![137]

The *Advocate* was not amused by the reception given Mitchell: "He was received in St. John's as something of a national hero ... others have defeated Prime Ministers and made far less of it." Editor Jack Scammell recounted the story of Walter Monroe's defeat at the hands of John Scammell, "a fisherman's son," in Bonavista

---

136 *Evening Telegram*, June 15, 1932.

137 Rudyard Kipling, "Recessional," in *The Literature of England*, ed. George K. Anderson and William E. Buckler (Glenview, IL: Scott, Foresman and Company, 1967), 1134.

Centre in 1928: "The fisherman's son took his victory modestly ... and had nothing further to say about Mr. Monroe further than calling him 'Mr. Monroe' and 'a gentleman withal.'" Although the *Advocate* had not officially taken a partisan side in the 1932 campaign, strong anti-Alderdice sentiments rumbled beneath the surface. The paper's writers were offended that Alderdice had called Sir Richard "a dragon" during his speech congratulating Mitchell: "We submit that such an expression was entirely uncalled for ... It is not Christian-like to gloat over an enemy's defeat, or glory in one's own successes."[138]

The final election results had not even been tallied when the financial advisor and deputy minister of finance, who had been seconded to Newfoundland from the UK Treasury, published his report on the state of Newfoundland's finances. J.H. Penson blamed many of Newfoundland's account problems on the "catastrophic fall in the price of fish [in 1931]" and exchange rate fluctuations which reduced the dollar amounts paid for Newfoundland cod. He also noted that "Newfoundland has been setting her financial house in order," and projected a balanced budget for the year starting July 1, 1932. Penson also underlined the Treasury control that Britain could now exert over the spending of money from the Newfoundland Treasury. The "powers and position of Controller of the Treasury ... cannot be removed from office except for an address to the two houses of the Legislature, and the appointment is one for which in the future, the recommendation of the Imperial Government will be sought."[139]

Quelling any doubt that the new government in St. John's would have to make unpopular decisions, Penson noted that "there

---

138 *Advocate*, June 17, 1932.
139 *Evening Telegram*, June 13, 1932.

are opportunities for economy which have still to be exploited." Still, apart from the reorganization of the public service which he believed would bring "increased efficiency and reduced cost," Penson confidently predicted "creation of a surplus [that would be] used to finance the redemption of debt." As further proof of his buoyant prediction, he concluded that "there is no reason why this should not be possible at a comparatively early date."[140]

With the election over, it was time for reflection and warning. "Newfoundlanders have taken the first step to save Newfoundland's reputation," the *Telegram* stressed, and asked the public to "show the patience that will be required during the period of convalescence."[141]

---

140 Ibid.
141 Ibid.

CHAPTER 5

Into the Gale

At the last session of the House, I was censuring the Government
for not taking notice of the impending gale. We have a hard road
to travel. The innocent will suffer with the guilty ...
—Frederick Alderdice, Leader of the Opposition, February 4, 1932

Almost immediately after being sworn into office, Alderdice came face to face with the full extent of Newfoundland's desperate fiscal position. The government was operating, but it was effectively broke. Revenue did not come close to keeping up with expenses and, as it had been almost every year since 1920-21, it was necessary to borrow to pay the interest on the public debt. The average annual deficit in the 12 years from 1920-21 to 1930-31 was $2 million.[142] By 1931, customs receipts, which made up the main source of government income, brought in $2 million less than projected. Debt costs, meanwhile, were $4,731,571 and would increase by another $400,000 in the next year. The government estimated that, by 1933, paying interest costs on the debt would consume 60 cents of every dollar the Treasury collected.

---

142 *Amulree Report*, 130.

During the 1932 election campaign, Alderdice and the UNP promised that within three months of their victory, laid-off factory workers in St. John's would be back on the job, and their factories working "at least three-quarters full time." Whether they believed such words and promises, no one will know. But the words would have brought comfort, especially in St. John's and some of the outlying areas in Conception Bay, where hundreds of people were out of work.

Once in office, Alderdice's government turned its attention inward, as it attempted to understand the shape and scope of Newfoundland's financial quagmire and to find a way to deal with it. On the expenditure side, salaries and pensions were slashed; on the revenue side, customs duties were increased. These decisions mirrored the unsuccessful steps Squires had taken. Days after taking over the reins of power, the Alderdice administration embarked on a program of austerity that left few government services untouched.

The first target was the Department of Posts and Telegraphs, the largest department in the government, with offices scattered in towns and communities throughout the island. Alderdice hoped the department would start balancing its accounts, and a subcommittee he appointed under Secretary of State Puddester was expected to produce quick results. After just three weeks, the committee made the first of numerous recommendations to shutter small post offices. In its July 18, 1932, meeting, Cabinet decided that the office at Admiral's Cove was "not necessary," and should be closed—while that at Cape Race should stay open, because it made money for the government, based on $150 in postage stamp sales and $500 in money orders. After paying the postmistress an annual salary of $36, a profit of $40 was realized. Suspicion that the department was poorly managed led to the Post Office Auditor and Inspector being "recalled to town" and given two weeks' notice "that his services [would] no longer be required."

By early September, Cabinet had closed 24 post offices and reduced salaries in line with government-wide cuts. At the September 24 Cabinet meeting, Puddester presented a list of 69 additional post offices to be closed, three to be consolidated with telegraph offices, and one to be combined with a telephone office. Six people would lose their jobs. It was also acknowledged at that meeting that several of that summer's decisions to close post offices had to be reversed. Cabinet agreed that certain post offices would be reopened and "some salaries increased in line with the amount of business." However, by October 14, Puddester's committee had listed another 29 post offices to be closed. The operator and postmistress at Baine Harbour had her annual salary reduced from $420 to $300, and the operator of the telegraph office at Exploits, from $540 to $500. Few escaped the cuts. The postmistress at Harbour Mille had her annual pay reduced from $45.10 to $30.[143]

The Alderdice government seemed intent on keeping open only those post offices that showed a profit, or those that were absolutely necessary—a deviation from Squires's strategy. In March 1932, Squires had told the House that there was no reason the postal department "should not make both ends meet," but he eschewed a policy that demanded that every office pay its own way, noting that "the service is a country-wide service [and that] not every individual Port Office or Telegraph Office can be made to yield a net revenue."[144] Where Squires took a kid-glove approach, Alderdice did major surgery. In the process, he reduced total

143 The Rooms Provincial Archives of Newfoundland and Labrador, GN/9.36, Cabinet Minutes, October 14, 1932.

144 *Proceedings*, Budget Speech, Sir Richard Squires, March 1, 1932, 13.

spending on the department from more than $1 million to $741,000; the number of post offices declined from 663 in 1931 to 313 in 1933 and telegraph offices from 71 in 1931 to 31 in 1933.[145] The government also implemented other charges, including an increase in some postage rates in 1932.

Some of these decisions would later be reversed. The February 20, 1933, Cabinet meeting was set to rectify those decisions, including an adjustment of the postage rate for newspapers and advertising matter. For example, the government had raised the postage rate for newspapers and advertising to 1 cent a pound. That decision actually reduced business for the post office, as several firms found other ways to distribute material that had previously gone through the mail. Alderdice, forced to backtrack, cut the rate for advertising matter by 40 per cent, to 60 cents per 100 pounds. Cabinet acknowledged that "certain advertising matter … [that was] was discontinued under the high rate, will probably be resumed under the reduced rate … and there will be no loss in receipts."

The new government made other missteps in trying to wring revenue from the postal service. The decision to increase letter postage from 2 to 3 cents, made in Alderdice's first weeks in office, backfired almost immediately. Such a measure had little impact in rural areas, since mail was virtually the only way to communicate with other parts of Newfoundland. But that was not the case in St. John's. In the legislature on April 25, 1933, Alderdice told MHAs that the post office gained $25,000 from the increase in the outports but lost $15,000 in St. John's. Large companies such as Light and Power, telephone companies, and rent collectors "ordered messengers to carry around their letters instead of posting their letters." Alderdice announced that the letter rate increase

---

145 *Amulree Report*, ch. II, para. 29.

would be reversed to 2 cents in "St. John's and all towns." The higher postal rate stayed in place in the outports.

The government also reversed its decisions on certain salary cuts. Two messengers from the Customs Department in St. John's "who are engaged in the constant transport of money to the Bank, and other responsible work" had their salaries "put back to $900 per annum." Similarly, for some telegraph workers and postmistresses "the present salaries fixed under the retrenchment measures made too drastic a cut in view of the importance of the Settlements, and the value of business handled by the officials." Accordingly, the annual salary for people running the post offices in various communities was raised: Port Union from $720 to $900; Green's Harbour, $120 to $200; Heart's Desire, $54 to $96; Heart's Delight, $120 to $200; and Stone's Cove, $120 to $240. Even with these reversals, however, the postal and telegraphs department was being cut down to a size more closely tied to the revenue it produced.[146]

The postal and telegraphs department cuts were part of a government-wide austerity program that identified savings from two main sources: the closing of offices and a reduction in salaries across the civil service. The Alderdice government made across-the-board cuts in all departments three weeks after being sworn in. That decision identified $145,436 in savings, but more trimming lay ahead. Few parts of the government were untouched. Alderdice believed that politicians should lead by example, and much was made of the $17,000 cut to the legislative budget. MHA sessional pay was reduced from $1,000 to $750; members of the appointed Legislative Council had theirs cut by $100 to $50 each; the Speaker's pay was reduced by $250; and the Law Clerk's position

---

146 The Rooms Provincial Archives of Newfoundland and Labrador, GN/9.36, Cabinet Minutes, February 20, 1933.

eliminated, saving another $300 per year. The government proposed saving $2,500 a year by trimming judges' salaries by 12.5 per cent. The bulk of the savings, however, came from government departments, and included a proposal to eliminate the $10,000 annual grant to the International Grenfell Association (IGA) at St. Anthony.[147] This was amended to a $2,500 cut after several petitions from White Bay area residents served by the IGA and Sir Wilfred Grenfell's opinion that "the absolute cutting of all assistance ... seems like a censure on the work of the Grenfell Mission."[148] The government also announced that it was shutting down the High Commissioner's Office in London, at a savings of $10,650. This decision was reversed 12 days later, on August 2.

Pensioners, many collecting benefits after only 10 years of service, had those benefits cut. Pensions were an especially hard hit on the Treasury, since, in the absence of a contributory pension plan, benefits were paid out of general revenues. Alderdice proposed a sliding scale of cuts based on income; the pensions of retirees at lower salaries were cut by 20 per cent; those at higher salaries could have theirs cut by as much as 45 per cent. Cabinet approved the cuts from a list provided by senior public servants. The former customs officer in the port at Lamaline, whose pension after 12 years of service was $222.48, had that amount reduced to $180, a 20 per cent cut. The housekeeper at the Customs House, with 21 years of service, had her annual pension reduced from $543 to just over $380.[149]

---

147 Ibid., Cabinet Minutes, Proceedings of Council, No. 36, July 20, 1932.

148 Hiller, ed., *Debates*, June 26, 1933, 1:321. The quotation from Alderdice was in response to several petitions from Joseph Moore, White Bay MHA, requesting that the government reverse the budget decision to eliminate the annual grant to the IGA.

149 The Rooms Provincial Archives of Newfoundland and Labrador, GN/9.36, Cabinet Minutes, July 26, 1932.

Pensions for World War I veterans were reduced by 15 to 30 per cent.[150] Those living outside of Newfoundland were affected even more drastically; their benefits were reduced by one-third. Most were not in the position of R.B. Herder of the *Telegram* newspaper family, who informed the Board of Pension Commissioners that he was "foregoing his claim as a War Pensioner at this time because of the financial condition of the country." The Cabinet decided to send Herder a "special letter of thanks and appreciation ... in respect of his patriotic action."[151]

In time, the government was moved to "readjust" some of the cuts to veterans, because of "special cases." In his 1933 budget speech, Alderdice noted that cuts were made with "great regret" and set aside "a larger contribution ... under the heading of Compassionate Allowance to War Veterans."[152] Despite his concern for the veterans, Alderdice did not reverse his position on pension cuts overall. He told the House on July 3, 1933, that "the pension should only be for a man who is worn out in the service." A civil servant who had worked for 20 to 25 years, in good health, and "well able to support himself" should not be entitled to a pension. He also introduced the idea that "pensions ought to be contributory [and added that] perhaps before next year," the government would bring such a measure before the House. Alderdice also felt that in rural Newfoundland, where there were few government jobs or other sources of stable employment, government pensions led to unnecessary friction with St. John's. He concluded that "pensions are far too high [and] they have caused a great deal of

---

150 Ibid., October 1, 1932.

151 Ibid., October 14, 1932.

152 *Proceedings*, Budget Speech, June 29, 1933, 278.

dissatisfaction in the outports."[153]

And yet, despite all the effort that went into cutting costs, the government's fiscal position continued to worsen. In part, this was due to an increasing need for public relief. Alderdice appointed himself to a subcommittee to discuss "the future policy in relation to the question of relief." Three weeks into his government's term of office, officials determined "that a larger amount ... would be required" for able-bodied relief than the $50,000 set aside in Squires's spring 1932 budget. In September, the deputy minister of finance clarified in a memorandum to Alderdice that the Dominion's finances were deteriorating steadily. Without further reductions in expenditure, he wrote, it would not be possible to "meet the charges of the Public Service." The only place to find the money was in the budget for salaries and pensions. At its September 15, 1932, Cabinet meeting, the government ordered a 10 per cent cut in salaries, hoping to save $190,000.

Alderdice's approach to government budgeting was founded on basic conservative principles of independence and doing the best with the available resources. In his Christmas message printed in the *Newfoundland Quarterly* in December 1932, Alderdice called for "a revival of the pioneer spirit with which our forefathers faced the reality of life," and implored people to remember the importance of "Diligence, Thrift and Self-Reliance."[154]

Alderdice believed that all arms of the government had to show the banks they were committed to cost-cutting. During the budget debate on June 27, 1933, Opposition leader Gordon Bradley suggested that cuts to government salaries would backfire, especially

---

153 *Proceedings*, July 3, 1933.

154 "A Christmas Message from the Prime Minister," *Newfoundland Quarterly* 32.3 (December 1932), 10.

reductions in the salaries of senior officials, citing the case of the government's chief accountant, whose salary had been cut from $2,700 to $2,300 a year. "He will be more than an ordinary man if he does not resent that," Bradley told Alderdice. Alderdice expressed concern about what the bondholders might think if they perceived that Newfoundland was making a half-hearted attempt to cut costs. "If we keep salaries at the highest level," he explained, "our debtors will say, and justly so, that we are not putting into effect the practical economy that is so necessary these days." He concluded: "We are compelled to cut down our estimates as much as we can ... we have to show our bondholders by making an honest effort to meet the situation."

No department was spared by Alderdice and his Cabinet. The Public Health Department had lost more than 10 per cent of its budget in two years, but the government believed there was room for more efficiencies. In the debate on the 1933 budget on June 27, Puddester claimed that 80 per cent of admissions to the General Hospital in St. John's from January to May were "absolutely not necessary." One man, fed "a single diet" for 86 days, "could have been looked after by the resident doctor." Puddester told the House that the General Hospital was treating people who did not need surgery, that $67,000 of its costs was the result of looking after the poor, including $6,000 "for looking after poor maternity cases." He called for "fair treatment" from outport doctors, whom he claimed were too quick to send patients to St. John's. "If they try to perform minor operations [in the outports] there will be no necessity whatsoever for sending patients into St. John's, for example, to have tonsils removed from a child."[155]

The government also tried to extract more from taxpayers for

155 *Proceedings*, June 27, 1933.

what it considered worthwhile projects. One measure was a 1-cent-per-gallon import duty on gasoline and kerosene. Alderdice, who doubled as minister of finance, brought the measure to the House for debate on July 5, 1933: the tax was expected to raise between $35,000 and $40,000. This revenue, he promised, would be "earmarked for the purposes of keeping the Highroads in some sort of repair." Opposition leader Bradley countered that the tax on gasoline should be 2 cents per gallon and levied only in places where people actually had highroads. He told Alderdice it seemed unfair to tax people in many outport places "where there is not the shadow of a Highroad." A 2-cent-per-gallon increase had been approved by Cabinet on May 16, but when the budget appeared in June, this had been reduced to 1 cent. Bradley's petition fell on deaf ears.

Customs duties were the principal source of revenue for the government and were applied on nearly every item shipped into Newfoundland, including some food. Frequent appeals were made to the government to allow tariff-free imports of certain goods, including gifts for religious orders. In January 1933, St. Bonaventure's College was eager to receive a $1,300 organ donated for use at the school. The usual request to the government to waive the duty was made, but Cabinet decided that a flat rate of $250 must be paid, just under 20 per cent of the item's value. Ten religious pictures to be displayed at convents in Newfoundland were allowed in at a duty of 15 per cent. Cabinet gave approval for a memorial window to be imported for use at Queen's College at a duty of 7.5 per cent.

Some exemptions, however, were granted. On March 23, 1933, Cabinet approved the duty-free import of machinery to be used in "experimental mining operations at St. Lawrence," but it ruled that regular rates would apply to the import of motor trucks for the operation. It also allowed the Italian Air Force to import

400 cylinders of hydrogen duty-free for the planned trip of its seaplanes to Cartwright and Harbour Grace in June and July 1933. It later extended more courtesies to the Italians by waiving the collection of gas royalties on their flights. In 1932, Alderdice joined the other British Empire leaders for the Imperial Conference in Ottawa. These conferences, which began in 1907, brought together heads of government in the British Empire to discuss common issues, usually involving defence and the economy. The principal outcome of the 1932 gathering was the empire preference tariff, brought in to encourage trading within the British Empire, and to lower tariffs on Empire-produced goods. But the application of the tariff caused problems in Newfoundland because of the country's long-standing trading practices with the US. Bradley forced Alderdice to admit to the problem during the budget debate in July 1933. Specifically, the issue was the tariff on cordage, including ropes and twines, and that British-made products were being given an advantage over products from the US. "If the lines are imported from the U.S.A., the price is higher?" Bradley asked. "Yes, the United Kingdom gets a 10 per cent preference," Alderdice replied. "The point I make is this," Bradley continued, "if a fisherman wants to use cordage as far as American cordage is concerned, he had to pay the additional duty." The Liberal leader wanted to embarrass Alderdice for having agreed to the tariff at the Ottawa talks without extracting a promise from the British to replace imported European ore with iron ore from Bell Island in return: "That is an additional tax on one of the main utilities in the production of our staple product, and I do not think it should be implemented until we get an advantageous proposition for our Wabana ore."[156]

---

156 Hiller, ed., *Debates*, May 16, 1933, 2:175–76.

Bradley scored points but little else in the debate on the *Bill to Control Alcoholic Liquors*. The issue was the government's intention to give police officers the right to stop any vehicle travelling on public highroads and for them to have the right to search for smuggled alcohol. "Not to mince matters," the acting justice minister, William J. Browne, told the House, "it is a well known fact that there is considerable [alcohol and tobacco] smuggl[ed] over the Whitbourne and Salmonier roads ..." The scope of the problem was so large that "the tobacco factory [practically] had to close down," but, he added, "the police ... now have their finger on this unlawful trade ... and it is for the purposes of prevention that these powers are now being asked for." Bradley acknowledged the loss of revenue for the cash-strapped government but argued there was a far more important right at risk if officers were given extended powers to stop any vehicle they wished. "Unless an officer of the law has reasonable grounds for suspecting that any particular individual is breaking the law, he has no right to interfere," Bradley argued. "Under this Section, he can go out on the road and hold up every motor car, every horse car, every carriage, every hen cart, every child with a wheelbarrow that passes along the road, without any reason whatsoever."[157]

Value for money took on new meaning as the Alderdice government tried delivering essential services at the lowest possible cost. For example, when the Opposition claimed that too many magistrates had been appointed, Justice Minister Emerson pointed out it was government policy to combine the positions of magistrate and medical doctor. Attracting doctors to certain areas was a challenge, he told the House, and "[i]n order to overcome that difficulty, the practice has been to make a grant out of the

---

157 Ibid., 2:177.

Magistrate's vote and appoint a doctor who will act as a Magistrate as well." In 1933, there were 83 doctors in Newfoundland, 36 fewer than two decades earlier.[158]

The civil service and department heads had little discretionary authority; virtually all government decisions were made by Cabinet. This was a significant distraction for ministers, given the major matters of reform and economic reconstruction that faced Newfoundland. Cabinet dealt with all financial issues, large and small. On January 30, 1933, ministers recognized the "exceptional circumstances and the splendid work" of postal workers during the busy Christmas season, and were asked to "pay each of the men ... the sum of $5.00" for the overtime they had worked. In early May 1933, Cabinet had to approve a request to allow a former soldier with the Royal Newfoundland Regiment to move his furniture back to Newfoundland duty-free, after he was unable to find work to support his wife and child in Montreal. Cabinet made the routine decisions that a modern civil service would ordinarily make, including agreeing to the duty-free entry of potato seed "for a man who's giving them away free of charge." It also waived postage for the IGA to send parcels of clothing to people in Labrador and White Bay.

In the battle to control costs and maximize revenue, few decisions showed empathy toward Newfoundland's suffering population. In early February 1933, Cabinet approved a plan to collect $1 a day from patients at the Riverhead Fever Hospital[159] "who are in

---

158 *Amulree Report*, ch. X, para. 593.

159 The Riverhead Hospital, which opened in May 1814, became the first civilian hospital in St. John's. With the departure of the British Garrison from St. John's in 1870, the military hospital on Forest Road was converted to a civilian hospital. Once this happened, the hospital at Riverhead (later known as St. John's Hospital) was used exclusively for people with typhus fever. Baker and Janet Pitt, "A History of Health Services in Newfoundland and Labrador to 1892," accessed July 5, 2014, http://www.ucs.mun.ca/~melbaker/PublicHealthNL.pdf.

a position to pay," and, on the same day, approved a plan from the Board of Liquor Control to have most employees work three fewer days a month, in order to save $520 a month in wages (the office staff was permitted to "keep full hours").

One item on the government's agenda had the potential to wipe out the public debt, but the sale or lease of Labrador did not happen. As early as 1927 (when Newfoundland's debt was $72 million), a proposal came from Fred Borden in Boston, who claimed he had the banking support to pay $50 million to the Newfoundland government in return for the right to develop hydro power at Grand Falls in central Labrador and to access iron ore in western Labrador. In early 1928, the government rejected the Borden plan, since it was "impossible" for Colonial Secretary Sir John Bennett to evaluate "the practicality of [the] proposal, or whether it is sound financially."[160]

Some Canadian politicians also saw potential in Labrador. In 1932, a group of 18 Liberal-Conservative Members of Parliament tried unsuccessfully to persuade Prime Minister R.B. Bennett to buy Labrador. The MPs told Bennett they had "been shown evidence that Newfoundland is willing to sell the Labrador ... to Canada ..." The politicians were concerned that "alien groups" might reach agreement with Newfoundland before the Canadians, with the result that such a deal "would strike a deadly blow at the present mining, timber and electrical industries in Canada." They asked Bennett to hire engineering and financing experts to assess "the sources of revenue to be derived from the administration of Labrador by Canada," which would allow Newfoundland

160 The Rooms Provincial Archives of Newfoundland and Labrador, GN/8.255, Letter, Borden to Bennett, October 8, 1927; Bennett to Borden, March 8, 1928.

to "adjust her present unsatisfactory finances [and] complete Confederation, and secure control of our Atlantic seacoast."[161]

The intrigue about Labrador continued. In the summer of 1932, Alderdice signed a memorandum that would allow a British-backed syndicate under the chairmanship of E.W. Sutphen to develop Labrador on a 99-year lease in return for payments that would cover Newfoundland's annual debt payments.[162] The Pioneer Syndicate Plan was signed on August 18, 1932, but the timing was off: Newfoundland agreed to the Amulree Commission in the fall of 1932 and, by the spring of 1933, the Sutphen plan was on hold as the Royal Commission began its work. In April 1933, Sutphen wrote Alderdice and Amulree, declaring he was "prepared to carry out the Plan." But by December 1933, with the Newfoundland government having voted to end responsible government, Sutphen wrote Alderdice again that "it was decided that [he] was not to consider further any possible arrangements for covering Newfoundland's bond service deficit on January 1st."[163] Sutphen was optimistic that the Newfoundland government would be "reinstated" in 1936 and understood correctly that Alderdice, Emerson, and Puddester would be the Newfoundland commissioners in the new government. For better or worse, the "Labrador option" for solving Newfoundland's debt problems was abandoned.

---

161 Ibid., Letter from 18 Canadian MPs to Prime Minister R.B. Bennett, April 12, 1932.

162 Noel, *Politics in Newfoundland*, 205.

163 The Rooms Provincial Archives of Newfoundland and Labrador, GN/8.255, Letter, Sutphen to Alderdice, December 4, 1933.

CHAPTER 6

The Trouble with Fish

It gives us no pleasure to give our readers a report of the fish
markets, because there is nothing promising to report.

—*The Fishermen's Advocate*, August 3, 1932

Newfoundland's fishery and the uneven quality of fish being
exported were matters of grave concern for Newfoundland's
politicians and for fish agents in Europe in the early 1930s. In the
winter of 1933, Alderdice asked D. James Davies, Newfoundland's
High Commissioner to London, to take a deeper look into the issues.
That spring, as part of his inquiry, Davies toured key Newfoundland
fish markets on the continent. His report unsettled Alderdice.

As Davies undertook his investigation, the previous year's cod
remained in warehouses in all the important markets. In Oporto in
Portugal, "everybody expressed a preference for Newfoundland
fish, but every businessman considered it was high time to pay
some attention to our grading"; in Genoa, Italy, "Icelandic fish [was
found to be] absolutely on top, with [Newfoundland's] nowhere."[164]

---

164 The Rooms Provincial Archives of Newfoundland and Labrador,
    GN/8.251, Letter, D. James Davies to Alderdice, March 13, 1933.

Spreading fish on a flake to dry, Logy Bay, ca. 1930. *The Rooms Provincial Archives of Newfoundland and Labrador, VA 15a-13.4*

Fish flakes on Topsail Beach, ca. 1900. *ASC, Coll-137, 07.03.006*

It was a depressing indictment for Newfoundland's key export, and Alderdice was determined it should be addressed. But how? Who would lead the charge? Could the situation be fixed in time to make a difference to the faltering Newfoundland economy?

Newfoundland was settled because of the cod fishery, and the salt cod industry sustained permanent settlement for three centuries. In 1933, it was hard to overstate the value and importance of salt cod to Newfoundland. People in hundreds of outport communities gained their livelihood from cod, and merchants benefited too. Well-known Water Street merchants like Crosbie, Hickman, Job, and Winter bought salt cod from fishermen and, in return, outfitted them in fishing gear and food.

The value of Newfoundland cod exports declined after World War I, but nothing rivalled what happened in 1931-32. The total value of cod exports dropped to $5,036,715, even less than the value of salt cod exports from Newfoundland three decades before, in 1900-1901. Captain George Whiteley, who was elected in St. Barbe in 1932 for the UNP, told the legislature that fishermen received between $1.25 and $1.50 per quintal of fish in 1931, down from $3.50 to $6.50 a quintal the previous year.[165]

Newfoundland's principal markets for cod were Spain, Portugal, Greece, Brazil, and the West Indies. Those economies were also impacted by the Great Depression, and that affected their ability to buy salt cod from Newfoundland. Spain, for example, bought about 10 per cent of cod produced by inshore fishermen (shore cod) in Newfoundland and "50 per cent or more of our Labrador," according to a letter to Alderdice in December 1933 from the chair of the Saltfish Exportation Board. Yet, the cost of fish from Newfoundland varied with the rate of duty and the

---

165 *Proceedings*, June 8, 1933.

complex way in which it was calculated. Duties were charged in gold, to which the Spanish government added an extra charge. The price was then converted to paper money, which varied depending on its relationship to gold. In December 1933, the duty on a quintal of fish reached 29.90 paper pesetas, or about 26 cents. The board reported to Alderdice that "the present high rate of duty on our fish going into Spain is a matter of grave concern to the Trade and to the country at large."[166]

Currency issues also interfered with the export of cod to Brazil. Problems in the Brazilian market emerged days after Alderdice took office, as fishermen were in the midst of the fishing season. Fred Bradshaw of the Mutual Exporters Association, a group of Newfoundland fish merchants, wrote Alderdice on July 16, 1932, to complain that the Brazilian market situation was "more acute" than he had expected. A request for guaranteed payment for Newfoundland fish on arrival in Brazil "was definitely turned down by one of our banks on the 13th," and all bills maturing before August 31 were subject to an automatic delay of 15 days before payments would be made.[167] The situation in Brazil led to a vigorous letter-writing campaign between Alderdice and the Secretary of State for the Dominions in London and became an example of Newfoundland's deference to Britain on matters of foreign affairs. In a letter to the secretary on July 11, 1932, and in another dated August 30, Alderdice complained about the problem of being paid in sterling for shipments of fish to Brazil. He asked the secretary to instruct His Majesty's Consul at Rio to ensure that fish from Newfoundland

---

166 The Rooms Provincial Archives of Newfoundland and Labrador, GN/8.248, Letter, Saltfish Exportation Board to Alderdice, December 9, 1933.

167 Ibid., GN/8.241, Letter, Fred Bradshaw, Secretary of the Mutual Exporters Association, to Alderdice, July 16, 1932.

received priority treatment for early and full payment. The secretary was asked "to use his good offices to secure that cod-fish is placed on the essential list, a position to which its qualities and value to Brazil entitle it ..."[168] Alderdice had made the same argument to Brazil's Consul in St. John's, Dr. F.A. de Silviano-Brandao, stating that Newfoundland cod exporters were "finding considerable embarrassment in carrying on business ..."[169] The Consul replied in mid-July, promising to "do everything in [his] power to have a favourable and prompt answer."[170] Newfoundland was heavily dependent on exports. The value of salt cod was down (exports had declined from $16 million in 1928-29 to $6.3 million in 1931-32). Iron ore and paper shipments had also declined, affecting employment on Bell Island and in Grand Falls and Corner Brook. Exports kept Newfoundlanders in jobs, and those with reduced incomes, or no income at all, could hardly be counted on to support the local economy.

As the Great Depression set in, Newfoundland's purchasing power declined, and customs revenue, which represented about 70 per cent of the government's receipts, dropped precipitously, from $7.46 million in 1930-31 to $5.7 million in 1932-33. Despite the gloomy prospects, Alderdice's government was buoyed by the prospect of improving the market situation with a better fish product from Newfoundland. While catches had declined by about 25 per cent from 1927 to 1928 (1,609,243 quintals of cod that year compared to an average catch of 1,162,000 quintals from 1930 to 1932), the major problems were tied to quality and price and currency issues. Alderdice could do nothing about currency

---

168 Ibid., Letter, Alderdice to Dominions Office, August 30, 1932.

169 Ibid., Letter, Alderdice to Dr. F.A. de Silviano-Brandao, September 1, 1932.

170 Ibid., Letter, de Silviano-Brandao to Alderdice, September 3, 1932.

but he could address fish quality, and he believed that consistently high-calibre cod would raise prices in the European market. His vision was two-pronged: to establish an independent regulatory regime to control the production, culling, and export of fish and improve overall fish quality; and to support strong fisheries research capability in Newfoundland to capitalize on its adjacency to some of the world's largest groundfish stocks.

The Fishery Research Commission, which predated Alderdice's government, was a joint initiative of the UK, through the British Empire Marketing Board, and the government of Sir Richard Squires. Newfoundland and the UK each pledged to contribute half of the $50,000 in capital funds required to establish the Board, and they co-operated on recruiting a foremost Scottish fisheries scientist, Dr. Harold Thompson, who was offered $6,000 a year salary and an additional $2,000 annually in his five-year contract to compensate for the loss of his British Civil Service Pension rights. He was given first-class travel to Newfoundland for himself, as well as his wife and child, and promised the same deal if he returned to the UK within three months after his contract terms were satisfied.

The rationale for setting up the Fishery Research Commission was set out in a letter dated March 10, 1931, to the governor, from J.H. Thomas, Secretary of State for the Dominions. Thomas felt Newfoundlanders had a tendency to take a narrow view of fishery prospects, with little emphasis on research. Recalling research in the US which had led to the discovery of haddock stocks, he pointed out that "the circumstances controlling the availability of the raw material are equally deserving of attention."[171] In its first season, the Commission oversaw the first-ever assessment of fish stocks

171 Ibid., GN/8.252, Letter, Fishery Research Commission to Alderdice, [n.d.].

off the coast of Newfoundland. It operated a vessel for nine weeks and took "samples of marine types at almost 230 places with different kinds of gear," including otter trawls and various types of cheesecloth to determine "the relevant facts concerning the food animals present in Newfoundland waters."[172] Its research extended to the production of new fish products at its cannery in Bay Bulls: cod and smoked cod fillets, capelin and smoked capelin, fresh and smoked cod tongues, salmon and smoked salmon fillets, and fresh halibut fillets. "Trial cases" of these goods were sent to the UK, the US, and Canada. The Commission reported at its August 26, 1932, meeting that they had sent a "small case of canned products, caplin and cod (2 styles) and salmon" to Alderdice.

As important as the future of the fishery was, most Newfoundlanders were concerned about the present, and in 1932, the government was coming to the somber realization that Newfoundland was responsible for many of the problems it faced in the world's fish markets. That would not have been news to Coaker and members of the Fishermen's Union Trading Company, the commercial extension of the union he founded in 1908. The Trading Company, which operated retail stores and bought salt cod from its members, had grown to 40 stores in communities along the northeast coast by 1919 and grossed $3 million in annual sales. By 1932, it had fewer branch stores and premises, but it remained the practical and ideological alternative to merchants and the credit system. Coaker wrote late in 1932 that the FPU was "a tremendous undertaking … of immense value" to the fishermen and communities of the northeast coast "and it would be a national calamity if it ceased to continue."[173]

---

172 Ibid.

173 *Advocate*, November 2, 1932.

The FPU was its own salt-fish exporter and knew intimately the state of foreign markets. Union members knew that 1932 would not be a good year. As early as June 1932, Coaker published notes of a trip that winter to Greece. "The consumption of codfish in Greece" had grown by 35 per cent in the previous five years, he wrote, but "Newfoundland has not benefited by any of the increase and solely owing to the poor quality received."[174] Coaker included notes from a man he claimed was one of the largest fish buyers in Patras, a Greek city built around a centuries-old port. The unnamed buyer outlined five ways that Newfoundlanders could improve the quality of their exported fish: The cod must be properly salted "in order to look sound and white"; sorting it into grades should be "more careful and regular"; producers of Labrador fish must "pack them the way Iceland and France do," with 30 per cent in bales and barrels, and 40 per cent in casks; packing in casks "should be more careful to avoid formation of sunken surfaces which makes fish look bad"; and every package of fish from Newfoundland should "contain a quality guarantee and … the inspector's name."[175]

Coaker's report contained all the advice Newfoundland needed to protect and enhance its most valuable export and the industry that sustained the majority of its population. It was not new information; Coaker had also attempted fishery reform from 1919 to 1921, but had failed. His idealism of those years had turned to cynicism by the early 1930s. He warned that, unless the people who fished and prepared Labrador cod, and the exporters who sent it to market, "show[ed] more interest in the curing, the salting and packing, they [would] surely lose the sale of Labrador cod in Greece" to their competitors in Iceland. By early August 1932,

174 *Evening Telegram*, June 27, 1932.
175 Ibid.

when the majority of the shore and Labrador fisheries were over for the year and cod was being readied for market, industry players shifted their attention to the market and prices. On August 3, the *Advocate* reported that the Spanish market was handicapped "owing to a restriction on sending money abroad" and Italy was "expecting shipments without credit or payment" until the fish arrived in Italian ports. This meant that "fish dealers will get whatever fish dealers in Italy wish to pay when they get the fish at Naples." Conditions in Brazil, it pointed out, were similar to those the St. John's fish exporters reported to Alderdice in July: "Brazil will take fish if shippers take all the risk, and wait six months or more for payment ... conditions now point to more trouble in disposing of fish locally, and in foreign markets, than has been experienced in our generation."[176]

Fishermen worried about the price their catch would capture. At St. John's buyers offered $2 a quintal, and in September fishermen at Flat Islands "along with fishermen from other sections of Bonavista Bay" met and decided "to hold out for $2.50 a quintal for Labrador fish." A delegation went to St. John's to press their case with the exporters and Alderdice. They were unable to get the exporters to budge from $2 a quintal, and they failed to get Alderdice to intervene and influence the exporters to raise the price. The experience in St. John's prompted the *Advocate* to report that fishermen "think that the line between [the Water Street merchants and the government] is altogether too close [and] they alas, find themselves in the clutches of a Water Street combine which refuses to budge, confident that no drastic action is to be feared ..."[177]

---

176 *Advocate*, August 3, 1932.
177 Ibid., September 21, 1932.

One way the government could take action was by implementing changes to *The Saltfish Act*. The legislation called for enforcing an inspection system that would closely monitor the quality of fish for export. These changes had been approved by the legislature under the Squires government but had not yet been proclaimed into law. The Alderdice government had delayed implementing the changes for 1932, a decision the *Advocate* called "sickening." The paper asked: "What is the use of asking fishermen to be extra careful in making good fish because there is going to be an inspection ... when the whole thing is taken no notice of by anyone[?]" The insinuation was that an appointed "special committee of fish exporters" was responsible for the delay.[178]

Alderdice's plan for the fishery was a slow-moving strategy. Soon after taking office he appointed John Stone as Commissioner of Fisheries, on July 14. Stone was asked to give "special attention" to fisheries issues. In a letter to the Norwegian Consul General six months later, Alderdice said he was "taking steps" for the establishment of a "Fishery Bureau to control the standardization of codfish and the regulation of shipments."[179]

A series of reports, each sounding an alarm about the state of markets in Europe, arrived in the prime minister's office in early 1933 and gave new urgency to the need for fishery reform. In addition to Davies's report, Holmes and Company, a UK-based marketing company, also sent market intelligence from Oporto, Portugal, a week after Davies, asking Alderdice to appoint a government official to oversee Newfoundland cod exports:

---

178 Ibid., August 10, 1932.

179 The Rooms Provincial Archives of Newfoundland and Labrador, GN/8.251, Letter, Alderdice to Helmer Bryn, January 23, 1933.

The Newfoundland position here is getting daily more desperate, and if present conditions continue, the market will be lost to us. [A competent government representative] would create instant confidence and show the buyers that serious consideration was being given to the business.[180]

Three weeks later, Holmes wrote again, confident that Davies's visit to the European markets had had a positive effect. Buyers were "willing to hold off from heavy purchases" of Norwegian and Icelandic fish, he told Alderdice, to see if they could "expect better treatment from Newfoundland than [they had] in the past."[181] Alderdice replied that the government planned to appoint a representative to oversee Newfoundland fish in the export markets.[182]

From his office at the High Commission in London, Davies made an impassioned plea in a telegram to Alderdice on March 28, 1933: "Our lost market almost tragic. Absolutely convinced immediate steps be taken or expect further and greater losses this coming season."[183] Davies, especially concerned about markets for fish from Labrador, told Alderdice that it was necessary to give immediate attention to the state of fish from that region.

The barrage of reports to Alderdice continued unabated that spring, and they all carried the same message—Newfoundland fish exporters had to drastically change the way they did business, or their markets would be lost. Fish broker T.P.K. Tracey pointed to more trouble from Newfoundland's competitors: "Labrador style and wet salted fish from Iceland." Iceland had produced just

---

180 Ibid., Letter, Holmes and Co. Ltd. to Alderdice, March 21, 1933.

181 Ibid., April 13, 1933.

182 Ibid., Letter, Alderdice to Holmes and Co. Ltd., April 17, 1933.

183 Ibid., Letter, Davies to Alderdice, March 28, 1933.

23,523 quintals of Labrador-style salted fish in 1910; by 1932, it was sending 351,633 quintals into the market, a 15-fold increase in 22 years.[184] Each quintal of fish from Iceland displaced a quintal from Newfoundland. On May 17, Holmes described the sales of Newfoundland fish as "most unsatisfactory, due without doubt to inferior quality and higher price."[185]

Nearly a year after entering office, Alderdice and his government drew up legislation for a new fish export regulatory body: *An Act Relating to Salt Codfish* was introduced into the House of Assembly on June 8, 1933. Alderdice gave a fiery speech on why the legislation was necessary, telling the House he was "determined" to carry out the UNP's pre-election promise to reform the fishery. He described the fishery and agriculture as Newfoundland's principal industries and outlined why previous fishery reforms had failed. As for Coaker's reform plan of 1919–21, Alderdice referred to "several evils" that existed at the time, including price-fixing. Coaker's regulations "were not carried out impartially [and there was a] great deal of uneasiness and distrust." He dismissed the 1931 reforms initiated by the Squires administration as political posturing, recounting "the sad spectacle of the Minister of Marine and Fisheries inserting a section in the Bill so that it might be killed." The intent of Alderdice's fisheries Bill was to improve the quality of Newfoundland's fish exports: "we cannot succeed if the merchants do not work with us." Newfoundland, he insisted, should emulate Iceland, which had built a valuable fishery based on quality and, along with Norway, had emerged as Newfoundland's chief competitors in the European salt cod trade.[186]

---

184 Ibid., Report, T.P.K. Tracey to Alderdice, April 4, 1933.

185 Ibid., Holmes Market Report, May 17, 1933.

186 Hiller, ed., *Debates*, June 8, 1933, 2:246–50.

The new fisheries law recognized two bodies, the Salt Codfish Exporters Association (established under the 1931 Act) and the Salt Codfish Exportation Board. Made up of exporters, the Association's role was to decide who could be a fish exporter. Under the new Act, the Board was given the "opportunity of considering and discussing any proposed regulations." Differences of opinion with the Board would be put to the Cabinet for resolution. The Board, made up of not more than three people, was to be non-political and unconnected to any company or fish exporting firm. It had the power to hire staff who were expected to devote their "whole time to their duty" and to hold office at the behest of the government. The Board was vested with many powers, all intended to ensure that the export of cod would be a regulated, non-partisan effort, with full attention given to eradicating the problems Davies and Holmes and Company had reported to the prime minister. Among the Board's many powers was the authority to issue export licences as well as inspector and grading certificates; to determine the grades of fish for export and what fish could be sold to foreign countries; to license fish exporters and regulate their shipments; to decide the packaging for exported fish; to stop the export of ungraded or uninspected fish; and to levy a charge on each quintal to cover the cost of the administration of the Board.

On July 3, 1933, less than one month after the House had debated and approved the new fisheries law, Cabinet approved $450 in moving expenses for Davies to leave the position as High Commissioner in London and move his family to St. John's, where he would take up his duties as the first chair of the Salt Codfish Exportation Board.[187] Davies had taken on a considerable challenge.

187 The Rooms Provincial Archives of Newfoundland and Labrador, GN/9.36, Cabinet Minutes, July 3, 1933.

He had seen the conditions in the European market during his tour in the spring of 1933, but, as evidenced in his reports to Alderdice, he appeared to have the right amount of optimism and straight talk for the appointment. In his letters to Alderdice in the spring, he described the state of Newfoundland fish, and even the packaging it came in. He appealed for better packaging to protect fish, explaining that many of the wooden casks were broken on arrival because they were not assembled properly. Newfoundland cod might still be a sought-after commodity by the poor in Portugal and Greece, but with Iceland producing top-quality fish, most markets expected better than the fish Newfoundland provided. He told Alderdice that European consumers were interested in the appearance as well as the taste of the fish: "All the importers say that people have been educated to eat with their eyes and not with their palates." Still, Davies hoped that Newfoundland cod would become a sought-after commodity if it was certified by a government-appointed fish grader. He believed the Spanish market "could absorb an additional 80,000 quintals of prime Spanish fish [and] there might be a possibility of increasing our market very considerably."[188]

The Alderdice government investigated new markets for Labrador cod outside its traditional focus in Europe, the Caribbean, and South America. Alderdice wrote J.H. Thomas to ask the UK's Commercial Counsellor in Shanghai to inquire about selling Newfoundland salt cod in China. The answer was not encouraging. Unless salt cod could be exported at $25 to $40 a ton (equivalent to $1.25 to $1.50 a quintal), a similar price to that of British Columbia herring, "it would have a small chance of success." The Chinese market required "cheap"; "Labrador fish can hardly be

---

188 Ibid., GN/8.251, Letter, Davies to Alderdice, March 13, 1933.

expected to compete in price."[189]

Alderdice contacted the Norwegian government in July 1932 to inquire "whether it might not be to our mutual advantage [to have Newfoundland, Norway, and Iceland co-operate] for the purpose of stabilizing the export prices of salted cod fish." Helmer Bryn, the Norwegian Consul General in Montreal, replied six months later, on January 16, 1933. Bryn was eager to clarify that this would not be an attempt "to force higher prices ... but only to guard against unreasonable competition, which forced prices down to such a minimum that the fishermen did not receive adequate compensation for their work."[190] Bryn told Alderdice that the Norwegian Cod Exporters' Association was interested in the suggestion and would discuss it with Davies during his visit to Norway during his spring survey of European markets.[191] The issue may have made it onto the agenda in Norway, but it did not result in a plan or agreement.

Alderdice and the Newfoundland cod exporters were not willing to give up on the Brazilian market, despite the currency export restrictions. The UK's Commercial Secretary at the embassy in Rio reported to London (and through Middleton to Alderdice) in July 1932 on the "worsening state of affairs [where oil exporters were] threatening to send only what they can pay for [and newspapers were] faced with not getting newsprint unless they can pay cash in foreign exchange." The worry was that cod shipments to Brazil would be especially at risk. "Bacalhoa [salt cod] shipments are likely to be cut off; this is the food of the

---

189 Ibid., Letter, His Majesty's Commercial Counsellor, Shanghai, to Dominions Office, February 15, 1933.

190 Ibid., Letter, Alderdice to Bryn, January 13, 1933.

191 Ibid., Letter, Bryn to Alderdice, February 11, 1933.

working classes—and in many homes the only dish for the Friday feast."[192] Alderdice appealed to the Bank of Commerce in Ottawa for solutions. It recommended that Alderdice write a letter to the state of Pernambuco (the Brazilian destination for much of the Newfoundland salt cod), rather than the national government of Brazil and include "a draft of a petition to the Minister of Finance of the State of Pernambuco ... drawn up in Portuguese."[193]

The Brazilian Consul in St. John's did his best but told Alderdice that Newfoundland exporters would have to be patient: "The Government ... when the situation improves, will supply drafts through the Bank of Brazil for 25% of all amounts due invoices of merchandise monthly, until each invoice has been paid for ..."[194] The Consul said his government would "give due consideration to any concrete proposition concerning a commercial agreement between Newfoundland and Brazil ..." Alderdice replied on September 17 with his "regret that the reply is not more encouraging." He accepted the Consul's agreement to talk about trade relations.[195]

Newfoundland repeatedly petitioned the British Embassy in Rio de Janeiro for help getting payment for the island's fish exporters. Embassy officials reacted with growing frustration. In a letter on October 26, 1932, H. Murray Harvey, the embassy's Commercial Secretary, wrote that "these restrictions are inconvenient to Newfoundland exporters, but when their case is compared with that of other importers, the hardship assumes a relatively

---

192 Ibid., Letter, His Majesty's Charge d'Affaires, Rio de Janeiro, to Alderdice, July 1932.

193 Ibid., Letter, Bank of Commerce, Ottawa to Alderdice, August 20, 1933.

194 Ibid., Letter, de Silviano-Brandao to Alderdice, September 15, 1933.

195 Ibid., Letter, Alderdice to de Silviano-Brandao, September 17, 1933.

insignificant aspect ... (fuel oils, petrol, coal—not being paid at all)." Exchange requests from Newfoundland were being given fair treatment, Harvey said, adding that British-owned utilities, railways, and boards were in much worse shape than Newfoundland interests: "for months [they] have been unable to remit a penny of their accumulations for debenture interest, profits, etc. [and] during the last six months, they have not even been allowed to remit trifling sums to support members of their staff on leave." Harvey then warned: "I strongly advise against the proposal to make further representations to the Brazilian government of this subject [since] there is no remedy the government can apply."[196]

That appeared to be the case. The manager of the Canadian Bank of Commerce in St. John's wrote Alderdice in confidence "that all drafts of the syndicate of fishery firms shipping to Brazil go through us, and that on the whole, payments for the fish already sent to Brazil have been much better than was expected." He concluded, "as a matter of fact, those importing fish have been able so far to remit for it in sterling, within approximately sixty days."[197] Alderdice received a similar confidential letter on December 8, 1932, from the manager of the Bank of Montreal in St. John's, that "under all circumstances, that we have been receiving some preference in exchange remittances."[198]

On December 9, 1932, Alderdice received a letter from the Monroe Export Company, advising him to stop badgering the

196 Ibid., Memorandum No. 110, H. Murray Harvey, Commercial Secretary of British Embassy in Rio de Janeiro to Governor John Middleton, October 24, 1932.

197 Ibid., Letter, Manager, Bank of Commerce, St. John's to Alderdice, November 25, 1932.

198 Ibid., Letter, Manager, Bank of Montreal, St. John's to Alderdice, December 8, 1932.

Brazilians for payment. The Company concluded that, by late fall, payments were being deposited in an acceptable time frame and advised that "it would be a mistake to make further representation to the Brazilian Government."[199] The Bank of Nova concluded it "would be just as well to 'let sleeping dogs lie,' as Newfoundland appear[ed] to be getting, if anything, preferred treatment from Brazil."[200]

The Brazilian currency problem was solved by December 1932 and, in March 1933, Alderdice wrote Sir William Seeds, the UK ambassador in Rio de Janeiro, to introduce Newfoundland fish merchant Chesley A. Crosbie, who was "undertaking a commercial visit to Brazil for the purpose of increasing the trade between that country and Newfoundland."[201] Even so, the fundamental problems affecting Newfoundland's fishery—poor quality curing, lack of a uniform grading system, and uncoordinated marketing—would not be addressed until 1933.

---

199 Ibid., Letter, Monroe Export Company to Alderdice, December 9, 1932.

200 Ibid., Letter, Manager, Bank of Nova Scotia, St. John's, to Alderdice, December 9, 1932.

201 Ibid., Letter, Alderdice to Sir William Seeds, March 20, 1933.

CHAPTER 7

The Empire Backs Down

The Great Depression hit all of Newfoundland's main industries with a devastating impact, but none was hit harder than the iron ore mine on Bell Island. Production dropped considerably—1,547,895 tons of ore were produced in 1928, 1,516,999 tons in 1929, a high of 1,177,961 tons in 1930, and then a steep drop to only 275,000 tons anticipated in 1932. In normal times, the mine employed 2,200 people. By 1932 and 1933, with worldwide markets shrinking, those numbers plummeted:

> At the present time, owing to the depression, two of the four slopes are closed, and the remaining two are worked for only two days a week. Employment is thus available only for 1,100 men, or half the number usually engaged, and even these are at daily rates: miners receive from $4.75 to $2.76 a day, and general surfacemen average $2.55 a day, mechanics $3.55 a day.[202]

---

202 *Amulree Report*, ch. VII, para. 439.

A group of miners on ore trucks on Bell Island. *ASC, Coll-137, 32.01.002*

Loading iron ore from Scotia Pier, Bell Island, ca. 1930. *ASC, Coll-137, 10.13.001*

Alderdice had few opportunities to get away from work and the stresses that accompanied the onset of the Depression and Newfoundland's economic slide. He and his wife, Harriet, did take a holiday in late August 1933 to visit their daughter Doris and her family in Halifax. It was a short-lived respite from the worries of work; by the time he arrived at his destination, Alderdice had to deal with problems connected with a small shipment of iron ore from Bell Island. The government had arranged to ship the iron ore to Wales, in exchange for coal to be used by the Newfoundland Railway. The agreement was part of a long-running but futile attempt to get a toehold in the British market with "Empire" iron ore.

The Bell Island mine was owned by Dominion Iron and Steel Corporation (DOSCO). Most of DOSCO's international shipments from Bell Island ended up in the blast furnaces of Germany, and by the summer of 1933, the Germans had heard of the plan to "barter" the ore for Welsh coal. DOSCO president Sir Newton Moore sent a telegram to Alderdice, stating that the Germans believed the sale of the ore to the UK "was at [a] better price than [that] offered the Germans." Alderdice assured Moore that he had advised London to inform Newfoundland's agent of what to say to further German inquiries:

> ... he should intimate that this is not a normal business transaction, but rather an exchange of coal for ore, and that the price, whatever it may be, has no relation to the ordinary contract and is affected by other considerations.[203]

203 The Rooms Provincial Archives of Newfoundland and Labrador, GN/8.247, Letter, F.C. Alderdice to Sir Newton Moore, Halifax, August 31, 1933.

Bell Island was a large community in the early 1930s, with close to 6,000 residents. Miners, who also came from nearby communities in Conception Bay, worked six days a week for three weeks, returning home for Sundays. One weekend a month, they got both Saturday and Sunday off. Most miners, however, lived on Bell Island, and when work was scarce during the early 1930s, they supplemented their low incomes with food from their own gardens, ploughed by horses borrowed from the mining company.[204] Bell Island is only 3 kilometres wide and 6 kilometres long, but residents made the most of their small piece of land. In 1934, they produced 12,000 barrels of potatoes from 338 acres and 66,000 gallons of milk, much of this bounty the result of 771 acres planted with hay. Farming was a means of feeding a family, and while some families could even make a living off the land, most needed the cash incomes from their jobs in the mines.

Iron ore was first mined on Bell Island by the Nova Scotia Steel and Coal Company in 1895. The mines went through a succession of ownership and structural changes in nearly 40 years of operation. As the Depression seriously undercut industrial demand in the early 1930s, DOSCO tried desperate measures to increase production and sales. Miners heard tales of the extreme hardship in Europe from ore boat captains who reported seeing shipments from the previous year lying untouched on the docks of Holland and Germany.[205] On July 1, 1932, the mine cut wages by 3.5 per cent; this provoked a strike. The miners called on Alderdice's

---

204 Charlie Bown, "Farming on Bell Island," accessed March 1, 2014, www.bellisland.net.

205 Wendy Martin, *Once upon a Mine: Story of Pre-Confederation Mines on the Island of Newfoundland* (Montreal: Canadian Institute of Mining and Metallurgy, c.1983), ch. V, accessed January 15, 2014, http://www.heritage.nf.ca/environment/mine/introduction.html.

office to intercede and he asked the MHA for Harbour Main-Bell Island, Charles Furey, to meet with miners and the company. Furey thought he had a deal when he proposed three weeks' pay at the unreduced rate for workers. The company agreed, but the workers rejected the proposal.

Alderdice expressed hope that he could help fill the company's order books at the 1932 Imperial Conference in Ottawa. Alderdice proposed enlisting the help of British politicians to negotiate a sale of 1 million tons of ore to British steelmakers, the *Daily News* reported, and "if that were successful, Wabana would be in full swing again."[206]

But the miners issued a new threat on July 3. The mines at Bell Island tunnelled out under the sea, and constant effort was required to keep sea water out of the work areas. The workers declared that if there was no deal by 3 p.m. on July 4, they would use the sea as a weapon. The *Daily News* reported that the workers had decided "the pump men would be wound down ... the lower pumps would be covered with water in 48 hours, and in another 48 hours, the mine would fill and become closed indefinitely."[207]

Alderdice needed to buy some time to head off a disruption that would further weaken the economy. He wrote to DOSCO, asking that they "postpone [their decision] until the end of August, thus allowing the government opportunity to deal with the situation."[208] DOSCO cabled back that same day. "We have lost one dollar per ton, not including bond interest and depreciation on all ore produced this year," wrote H.J. Kelley of the Steelworks

---

206 *Daily News*, July 1932.

207 Ibid.

208 The Rooms Provincial Archives of Newfoundland and Labrador, GN/8.247, Telegram, Alderdice to H.J. Kelley, DOSCO, July 3, 1932.

in Sydney, adding that DOSCO was "not hopeful of any new business that [would] assist our operations this year."[209] According to the *Daily News* the mine manager at Bell Island "had no notification of any steamer coming … and did not know when there would be another." DOSCO officials believed that if the Newfoundland government could intervene with the UK government, the mine would find a market with steel producers in Britain. DOSCO enlisted Alderdice's assistance to further this goal, with the belief that the Empire would find extra value in trading with its oldest colony, and one of its newest Dominions. It would turn out to be an exhausting and frustrating appeal, exacerbated by retaliatory measures from traditional European producers.

Alderdice asked DOSCO to delay pay cuts at Bell Island in 1932 in part because he had faith that he would find a solution to the market problems besetting the mine at the Ottawa Imperial Conference that summer. As he cabled Kelley prior to leaving for Ottawa: "Have hopes we may be able to offer at Ottawa inducements whereby orders for ore may be obtained from British Steelmakers." Concerned about the impact of a pay cut on the workers and whether it would disrupt labour peace, he noted, "matters now in very critical condition and require very careful and prompt handling." He had considered adding another line to the cable —"Men claim suddenness of reduction gives them grounds grievance"—but crossed it out.[210]

DOSCO agreed to Alderdice's request to postpone pay cuts. On July 11, he expressed his gratitude to them for having "temporarily avoided a serious situation on the Island." He wanted them to go even further, requesting that the pay cut be shelved "for the

---

209 Ibid., Telegram, H.J. Kelley to Alderdice, July 3, 1932.
210 Ibid.

month of August" so that he could meet British officials in Ottawa to "promote the sales of Bell Island ore in Great Britain." The *Daily News* complimented Alderdice: "It is very gratifying to know that in the first outstanding problem the new Government has had to grapple with, both the people and the administration have been able to produce a satisfactory understanding in short order."[211]

Part of the deal to end the strike was an undertaking by MHAs Furey and Browne to "make an effort to have the royalty removed." The royalty was a 10-cent-a-ton levy implemented in the 1929-30 budget by Squires's Liberals.[212] The levy applied to the first 1 million tons of ore, and was reduced to 3 cents a ton on the next 500,000 tons. The tax added $115,000 to the public coffers in 1929-30.[213] Browne and Furey attended a tense meeting on Bell Island, where the situation was all the more difficult because the miners' representatives had been drinking. "God help you if you don't do something for the men," one miners' representative told Browne. Browne and Furey's job was made somewhat easier by the government's promise to send officials to Bell Island to assist people who had fallen on hard times. Browne left the meeting with the representatives and asked for "Ayes" and "Nayes" from the miners gathered outside, on removal of the 10 per cent royalty. With their acceptance, and the Bell Island agreement in his hand, Browne left the island at 6:45 p.m. and reported to a meeting of the Executive Council at Government House at 8 p.m. It is unclear whether he raised the matter of removing the 10-cent-a-ton royalty, but the

---

211 *Daily News*, July 5, 1932.

212 The royalty replaced a 25-cent-a-ton levy put in place in 1920, but the operator, British Empire Steel Corporation, and its successor, The National Trust Company, refused to pay, until Squires came to power in 1928 and implemented a new, lower rate.

213 *Journal of the House of Assembly*, Budget Speech, April 22, 1931, 237.

Daily News reported it was "understood" that he "may recommend this suggestion before the end of this month ..."[214]

The effort to find labour peace on Bell Island was noticed in Port Union. The *Advocate* was adamant that the government keep the iron ore royalty in place, advising it "not to throw away a dollar to obtain 80 cents." It reminded Alderdice that new taxes levied in the spring budget on provisions, gasoline, and kerosene had cost the Trading Company $30,000. The paper accused the owners of the Bell Island mines of "playing a game at a time when everyone is crushed with taxation."[215]

A week after the Bell Island problems were exposed, Alderdice boarded a train for Port aux Basques en route to meeting DOSCO officials in Sydney and then to Ottawa. The *Daily News* reported that Alderdice was "heartily cheered" as the train moved out, good wishes that could not hide the challenge he would face at the conference.

Alderdice cabled Harry Winter, who was acting prime minister while Alderdice was out of the country, from Montreal on July 24 to report on his meeting with DOSCO. "Am convinced company confronted with serious situation," he wrote, adding that the earlier the company could reduce its costs, "[the] greater likelihood [of] continued operations."[216] This cable represented a distinct change from the tone of the telegram to Kelley nearly two weeks previous, when Alderdice had pleaded for a delay in the pay cut at Bell Island. Alderdice's views had shifted after his meeting with DOSCO officials. He told Winter that the company's poor situation

---

214 *Daily News*, July 5, 1932.

215 *Advocate*, July 1932.

216 The Rooms Provincial Archives of Newfoundland and Labrador, GN/8.247, Telegram, F.C. Alderdice to Harry Winter, July 24, 1932.

"entails [a] paycut going into effect on August 1." Alderdice want-ed assurances from DOSCO "that present working hours should be continued until next May 1933," and, further, that DOSCO might offset reduced wages with price cuts at the company-owned store on Bell Island. DOSCO had not asked Alderdice for a cut in the export tax on its ore and, in any event, he was unwilling to diminish government revenue further, telling Winter that such a move would be "wrong in principle."

Winter had grave doubts about Alderdice's chances of get-ting Bell Island iron ore into Britain. In a letter to his friend and investment partner, John Gilbert Higgins, on August 9, Winter revealed he had received a wire from Alderdice in Ottawa: "[he] has good hopes [of something] worth while [from the confer-ence]. Which deepens my cynicism, which I have had from the beginning, that we will get nothing whatever <u>directly</u> beneficial from it at all."[217]

Alderdice expressed no such misgivings about the confer-ence. It must have been a relief for him to bask in its pomp and protocol. Although Newfoundland did not practice its own foreign policy, it was treated as an equal at the meeting with Em-pire leaders. Alderdice and his wife had been invited by Prime Minister Bennett to a dinner at the Chateau Laurier Hotel and by the Governor General and his wife to a Garden Party at Rideau Hall. Bennett was at the train station to welcome the Newfound-land prime minister to Canada's capital. Alderdice was impressed by the trappings of the Imperial Conference, telling the St. John's Rotary Club on his return, "I had quite a feeling of awe when I sat down in conference with men with world-wide reputations, men

---

217 ASC, Coll-087, Letter, H.A. Winter to John Gilbert Higgins, August 9, 1932.

who had the empire in the hallow of their hands."[218]

On July 15, as Alderdice was en route to Ottawa, the *Advocate* concluded that the Ottawa meetings would be a waste of time. "The Conference cannot, and will not, benefit Newfoundland. What the Conference will do is order Newfoundland to place an extra tax of ten percent or more on imports into this country from outside of the British Empire," thereby making Newfoundland goods more expensive for export. Alderdice would find little support to sell ore to England, as, it stated, "that has been attempted many times during the past twenty years, all to no avail."[219] The *Advocate*'s position on the Ottawa talks reflected its own deep experience in international trade. By contrast, the two St. John's dailies, parroting the prevailing political and business views in the capital, made little effort to analyze the issues of the day. The St. John's papers and the Board of Trade voiced equally optimistic views of what could be gained at the Ottawa conference, without much consideration of the potential downside for Newfoundland. "This conference is destined to be the greatest event of the century," claimed the Board, as it announced that it was sending three delegates, each of whom would pay his own expenses. The Board planned to promote the export of Bell Island ore "as much as possible" during the conference. The *Daily News* hoped for "a revival of German trade" to assist the mines at Bell Island, and that "Britain may be ready to give consideration to proposals herself to try out Newfoundland ore."

Anyone reading the *Daily News* might well conclude that Newfoundland was emerging from the Great Depression sooner than other parts of the world: "Reports of factories working full

218 "Hon. F.C. Alderdice's Address at Rotary Club: The Prime Minister Believes Great Good Will Accrue," *Newfoundland Quarterly* 32.2 (October 1932), 23–24.

219 *Advocate*, July 15, 1932.

time, of big turn over by dealers in the city, and of hopeful news from the fishery ... are giving a renewed buoyancy to business." The editorial spin was at odds with what appeared on the paper's news pages. Apart from the problems on Bell Island, hundreds of workers at the paper mill and associated operations in Corner Brook faced pay cuts. The International Paper Company cut wages by 10 per cent during the winter of 1932, reduced "the number of men at the paper machines" in April, and unilaterally announced another 10 per cent cut in wages on June 28 to be effective 10 days later. The paper's editorial assessment of a buoyant economy appeared at odds with the experience of Newfoundland workers.

The *Daily News* believed that Alderdice's approach to governing, along with the absence of self-minded politicians, would accomplish the dual goals of righting the economy and resolving the fiscal problems facing the government. It advocated for concessions, no matter how tough they were. It praised Alderdice for foregoing his $3,000 annual salary in the name of government austerity, noting that it was "an action in keeping with the inherent, straight-faced honour of the man" and underlining that his personal effort to control spending in the legislature contributed to $13,425 in savings in the House of Assembly vote. The paper did not mention that, by Newfoundland standards, Alderdice was a relatively wealthy man and the loss of $3,000 would not send him to the poorhouse.

At the end of July, Bell Island miners had to face the wage cuts that Alderdice and the government had managed to delay for a month. The *Daily News* called for calm, stating that "there is hope that out of the Empire Conference at Ottawa will emerge some help for Newfoundland, and particularly for its iron ore industry." Until then, it cautioned, "any action that might jeopardize the future would be very serious for the residents of the island." The August 2 *Daily News* expressed relief that the miners did not protest the wage cuts, and complimented them on "accepting an unpleasant situation quietly."[220] The paper supported the government's agenda to have few public voices of discontent in the country. When the government was publicly criticized—as it was during an outbreak of vandalism in St. John's by unemployed men in the summer of 1932—the perpetrators were quickly marginalized as a "group of young hooligans" who "reflected badly on the fair name of the city."[221]

Meanwhile, at the conference in Ottawa, the Newfoundland delegation held numerous meetings with British and Canadian officials in an effort to get preferential treatment for ore from Bell Island. Alderdice played all the angles. In a letter to the Canadian government, he advocated Newfoundland ore use in Canadian mills; to the British, he promoted a "British Empire Product [from] the only Empire mines producing iron ore wholly for export purposes." It was a hard and desperate sell. Britain had imported about 5 million tons of iron ore in 1927. In 1931, imports had declined to about 2 million tons. Alderdice promoted Bell Island ore as "superior to Alsace iron [and] equivalent to Spain['s],"[222] the major exporter to Britain. The Newfoundland strategy to get Bell Island iron ore into British steel mills was based on a combination of good old-fashioned political lobbying and appeals to the British sense of "fair play." Alderdice pleaded the case in a letter to J.H. Thomas, Secretary of State for the Dominions, telling him that miners were suffering, "work [was] limited to two days a week," and just two of the four mines were operating:

---

220 *Daily News*, August 2, 1932.

221 Ibid., July 26, 1932.

222 The Rooms Provincial Archives of Newfoundland and Labrador, GN/8.247, Letter, F.C. Alderdice to J.H. Thomas, August 13, 1932.

> The Delegation considers that a quota of at least 1,500,000 tons of ore a year in normal times should be granted by the United Kingdom to Wabana, equivalent to approximately 30% of British imports of ore.[223]

Three days later, Alderdice wrote to Walter Runciman, Britain's president of the Board of Trade, offering more specifics on what DOSCO was prepared to offer in ore shipments to Britain: 500,000 tons shipped between August and December 1932 and a similar amount each year until 1937. British steelmakers, then, would have a guaranteed supply of ore from Newfoundland. DOSCO would also cut its price from an earlier offer, which Alderdice deemed "a considerable reduction [and a] very considerable concession on the part of the Corporation ..." Even though Runciman was a Cabinet minister and undoubtedly influential in Britain's affairs, he was not in charge of the British steel industry. His response on August 17 was polite and understanding, but it was not what Alderdice and DOSCO wanted to hear:

> [He was] arranging for the representatives of the iron and steel industry in this country to have at once the order which you have tendered to me, and it would give me great satisfaction if business were to result. At the same, I am sure you will appreciate that the U.K. Delegation cannot do more than use their good offices with the iron and steel industry, for the reason which Sir Henry Fountain explained to you the other day.[224]

---

223 Ibid.

224 Ibid., Letter, Runciman to Alderdice, Ottawa, August 17, 1932.

When the conference ended on August 20, the British delegation prepared to leave for Quebec City to board the *Empress of Britain* for the trip home. Alderdice explained to the Canadian Press
what Newfoundland had gained from these meetings: Newfoundland businesses would gain from their ability to export fish, cod
liver oil, and chilled salmon into the UK and, he noted, "every influence [would] be used to persuade Iron-Masters to use Wabana ore."

Alderdice returned to Newfoundland without the coveted
deal to sell Bell Island ore, and the best he could report to the
Rotary Club in his September 1 speech was that the UK government had "promised ... they would use their influence" to get
British steelmakers to use Newfoundland ore. The problem, he
offered, was price: "I pointed out that it was not possible for our
people to mine ore in competition with Arabs in Algeria who can
live on a handful of grapes and a glass of water."[225]

Even the *Daily News* writers found it difficult to explain that
no deal had been made to sell iron ore to the British. Alderdice
had promised "tariff concessions" to the British if they took
100,000 tons of ore in 1932, and 500,000 tons a year until 1937,
and to effectively lessen duties on British goods by valuing the
pound sterling at $4.20 Canadian, about 60 cents less than the pre-
vailing exchange rate. The absence of a deal "might at first glance
seem problematical," but the newspaper banked on the reputation
of British politician Stanley Baldwin,[226] Board of Trade president
Walter Runciman, and J.H. Thomas, Secretary of State for the
Dominions. "Mr. Baldwin himself," the *Daily News* noted, "is an
ironmaster, [and Alderdice] feels so confident of the undertaking

---

225 "Hon. F.C. Alderdice's Address at Rotary Club," 23.

226 Lord President of the Council, highly influential because of Prime Minister
     Ramsay MacDonald's poor health.

that he confides to his colleagues here that he considers it practically equivalent to a firm sale." The truth was, the UK had never been anything other than a minor purchaser of ore from Bell Island—it did not purchase any iron ore from Bell Island in 1927, less than 2 per cent of the mine's output in 1928, and about 5 per cent in 1931.[227] The editorial injected a note of realism, noting that British ironmasters would have to be "sold on" Newfoundland ore and that such a deal would take some time to happen.

While the St. John's dailies gave Alderdice credit for trying to find new markets for Newfoundland ore, the *Advocate* was brutal in its assessment of the conference and its possible benefit to Newfoundland. After Alderdice gave his conference report in a September 1 address to the St. John's Rotary Club, which was also broadcast on radio, the *Advocate* stated that "Mr. Alderdice used very poor tact [leading people to conclude that] delegates ... paid more attention to the social functions than they did to the affairs of either the United Kingdom or the British Dominions."[228] It continued: "We can say that we must, unfortunately, think that Mr. Alderdice's address was probably the greatest proof that has yet been produced that so far as Newfoundland is concerned, the Imperial Conference is an outright failure."[229]

The chief outcome of the conference was "preferred trade" within the Empire, just as the *Advocate* had predicted in mid-July—reduced tariffs for trade within the Empire and high tariffs for trade without. The best Britain could do was to "recognize that an arrangement between the interests concerned for the importation into the United Kingdom of a substantial quantity of

---

227 *Amulree Report*, 441.
228 *Advocate*, September 7, 1932.
229 Ibid.

Wabana iron ore is of paramount importance to the economic life of Newfoundland." Alderdice boasted of the tariff protection he had obtained for cod liver oil and salmon, but that would not help Bell Island.

By late August, Alderdice was back in St. John's, the Ottawa dinners and garden parties a distant memory. On August 31, the mine manager at Bell Island forwarded a cable from Moore, DOSCO's president. The shipping season was winding down and Moore was "respectfully suggest[ing that the] British Government be urged to expedite arrangements discussed [in] Ottawa re: Wabana ore."[230] Alderdice urged patience, as he did not "care to embarrass them with further pressure" until government officials had the opportunity to meet with officials from the steel industry. "It occurs to me," Alderdice wrote, "that the London Office of your company might be of considerable assistance by getting in touch with the various Steel Masters, and putting every pressure on ..."[231]

The Great Depression had made life difficult for nearly every Newfoundlander, and local producers had to exploit every opportunity to sell any product or good. Alderdice wrote to the mine manager at Bell Island, inquiring about the company's annual use of "hay, potatoes, cabbage, turnips, and other vegetables in its stores. [He thought it was] quite possible that [their] entire needs in this direction can be supplied from local sources."[232]

By early October, with no sign that Britain's steel mills would accept its iron ore, DOSCO prepared to take desperate measures: it offered to sell 100,000 tons of ore at a "distressed price" to generate

---

230 The Rooms Provincial Archives of Newfoundland and Labrador, GN/8.247, Cable, Moore to Alderdice, August 31, 1932.

231 Ibid., Letter, Alderdice to Moore, September 2, 1932.

232 Ibid., Letter, Alderdice to Archibald, September 10, 1932.

cash flow, asking the government to help by waiving the 10-cent-a-ton royalty "on any quantity shipped next year." A further request was made to DOSCO's power supplier, Royal Securities Corporation of Montreal, to reduce the price of electricity by about $3,000 a month. If both parties could meet that demand, Moore said he would agree to reduce the price for each ton of ore by 20 per cent, from just over £11 to £9. Moore's goal was to "relieve the distress among the employees at Wabana [for] the ensuing season."[233]

The Newfoundland government met Moore's requests partway, and agreed to remit the 10-cent-a-ton royalty to DOSCO on 100,000 tons, worth $10,000 to the company, and Royal Securities Corporation agreed to cut power rates by 13 cents a ton, a savings of $13,000 to DOSCO. It was less than Moore had hoped for—he wanted the equivalent of a reduction of 39 cents a ton on the electricity bill—but he wrote Alderdice on October 17, 1932, that "under the circumstances, [he] felt there was no option but to accept."[234]

The Newfoundland government and Moore could make no headway in Britain. The steel masters responded to the hard-won DOSCO price cut by saying it was not enough. Moore cabled Captain Bullen of British Empire Steel Company Limited (BESCO) for him to pressure the government and the steel industry by having Conservative MP Sir Percy Hurd question the government in Parliament about "the necessity of safeguarding the iron ore supply for the Empire as jealously as copper."[235] But Britain's steel producers were not answerable to the government, and they could get a ready supply of iron ore from their traditional suppliers in Europe at substantially lower prices. Steel producers

---

233 Ibid., Letter, Moore to Alderdice, October 6, 1932.

234 Ibid., October 17, 1932.

235 Ibid., October 31, 1932.

in France, Germany, Belgium, and Luxembourg were resurrecting the steel cartel that had collapsed during the first years of the Great Depression. They proceeded to export iron ore to Britain at up to £1 a ton below the prices they charged other countries.

Alderdice expressed his disappointment at the effort to sell ore to Britain in a letter to Kelley in early December: "I am very much discouraged by the replies we are receiving from the U.K." Alderdice quoted from a letter from Stanley Baldwin, Lord President of the Council in the British government and a former steel master: "I am sorry the official reply [from the steel industry] being sent now has to be so discouraging ..."[236]

Moore was persistent. He travelled to Geneva and Germany to find new buyers for DOSCO's ore. He achieved an occasional success, including an order for three additional cargoes for Germany in early January 1933. On that trip, Moore retraced his steps to the UK, where he secured a "tentative proposition" for 40,000 tons with another buyer, which buoyed him somewhat. But he could not hide his disappointment at his reception in Britain, and at Newfoundland's agreement to exchange Newfoundland pit props for Welsh coal for the railway: "It has been a great disappointment to me that you found it necessary to take in any British coal, and the less coal we produce in Nova Scotia, the more difficult we find the task of financing the operation."[237]

Alderdice felt that he had few options with the British government and that he could only ask authorities to help with iron ore imports. At the same time, he appeared reluctant to raise the stakes with British steel producers. In response to an article in the publication *Canada* in early 1933, in which he was criticized by

---

236 Ibid., Letter, Alderdice to Kelley, December 9, 1932.

237 Ibid., Letter, Moore to Alderdice, January 6, 1932.

Participants in the Imperial Economic Conference, Ottawa, July 1932. Alderdice is seated, front row, seventh from right. Official Canadian Government photograph, Library and Archives Canada, R11954-4

Sir Julian Piggott of the British steel industry, Alderdice chose to reply privately to Piggott rather than write to the publication. "It would serve no good purpose," he wrote Moore on February 7, "to antagonize any of the principal Steel Masters to whom we come looking for business."[238] It was not the first time Alderdice took the less combative route. In the late fall of 1932, just months after the Imperial Conference, he was again prodded by a frustrated Moore to be more aggressive with British politicians on ore exports. Moore, receiving no result from his decision to cut prices for Bell Island ore, criticized the government in London:

> Cable Baldwin and Thomas, pointing out the attitude of Steel Masters of Great Britain, and the lack of support extended by the British Government practically amounted to a breach of the arrangements agreed to in Ottawa, and that it has created a most unfortunate impression here ...[239]

---

238 Ibid., Letter, Alderdice to Moore, February 7, 1933.

239 Ibid., Letter, Moore to Alderdice, November 9, 1932.

In his cabled reply, Alderdice advocated a less provocative approach, again displaying great deference to Britain and recommending that Moore delay making accusations:

> It is evident steel people want everything without giving any return [stop] Recommend refraining making any charge bad faith UK Government pending my appeal Baldwin and Thomas.[240]

Alderdice never intimated it in his letters, but he likely grew as frustrated with the frequent communications from Moore as he was with the shortage of orders for ore.

Opposition leader Gordon Bradley also challenged Alderdice on the outcome of the conference, proclaiming to the legislature that the Ottawa tariff agreement was "simply a continuation of the tariff wall-building scheme. I do not believe in creating artificial trade channels."[241] Although Alderdice had little success in Ottawa, and the Bell Island ore was one glaring example, he defined and defended the Ottawa deal in Imperial terms and believed that the agreement with the Empire would bring dividends:

> I glory in the fact that we will have closer relations within the Empire … we all have English blood in our veins and I am sure we would rather trade with Englishmen than Chinamen … I believe that in two years, [we] will be able to increase our cod liver export by 50-percent, and in addition to that, within three years we will be selling 500,000 to 3,000,000 tons of ore to the United Kingdom.[242]

---

240 Ibid., Cable, Alderdice to Moore, November 9, 1932.

241 *Proceedings*, June 29, 1933.

242 Ibid.

Alderdice's fierce loyalty to the Empire precluded any criticism of Britain on iron ore or any other issue. The mine at Bell Island, which had a payroll of $2 million in 1930, was paying out $500,000 in wages two years later in 1932. It would be many years before production increased. Ironically, it was Germany's demand for iron ore in the build-up of its military arsenal in the years before World War II, and not the benevolence of the British Empire, that brought prosperity to the mines. By 1938, DOSCO had opened up all four Wabana mines to keep up with the demand from Germany. The last shipment to Germany came days before the Nazis invaded Poland on September 1, 1939.[243]

---

243 Martin, *Once upon a Mine*, ch. V.

CHAPTER 8

Newfoundland
and the World

Will you be in London for the World Economic Conference?
If so, I hope to see you as I will again be representing South Africa.
—N.C. Havenga to Frederick Alderdice, May 1933

The Alderdice government rolled out the red carpet for the Italians in August 1933. Italian Air Minister General Italo Balboa led an armada of 24 planes that made two stops in Newfoundland: one in Cartwright, Labrador, on its way to the Century of Progress Exhibition in Chicago; and another on its return in late July at Shoal Harbour near Clarenville. The cash-strapped Dominion of Newfoundland, eager to keep up salt cod shipments in Europe, including in Italy, began its display of diplomatic hospitality months earlier on May 6, when Cabinet waived the collection of royalties on the gas the Italians would use during their summer stopover.

Balboa and the officers of the Royal Italian Air Squadron took the train from Clarenville to St. John's, where Alderdice and the government honoured them at a luncheon at the Newfoundland Hotel on August 5, 1933. The Italians and their hosts dined on breaded cod steaks, spring lamb chops, and roast turkey, and finished with peach melba, crackers and cheese, and coffee. Alderdice proposed toasts to the king, Victor Emmanuel, and Il Duce, Benito Mussolini. Balboa reciprocated with a toast to King George V. This ceremony was one of the few occasions when Newfoundland hosted high-profile foreign visitors.

Newfoundland's status as an equal to all the other governments in the Commonwealth had been confirmed in the 1926 Balfour Declaration, and the country could have begun practising its own foreign relations under provisions of the Statute of Westminster, 1931, which gave self-governing dominions control over domestic and foreign affairs. The 1931 Statute applied automatically to Canada, the Irish Free State, and South Africa. Australia, New Zealand, and Newfoundland were covered in Section 10: they had to adopt the Statute before it applied. Newfoundland showed no desire to do that and, as a result, primarily restricted its external affairs role to its relationship with other self-governing Dominions, primarily Canada. Britain and Newfoundland agreed on the island's constitutional status, though it was a curiosity for some Empire nations.

In 1929, three years after the Balfour Declaration stated that Britain and the Dominions were autonomous,[244] the Union of South Africa wrote to the Dominions Office in London to inquire into "the precise position of Newfoundland as a Dominion." In its reply, the Office stated that "His Majesty's Government in

---

244 The Balfour Declaration of 1926 was approved at the Imperial Conference in London. In declaring the autonomous nature of Britain and the Dominions, it stated: "They are autonomous Communities within the British Empire, equal in status, in no way subordinate one to another in any aspect of their domestic or external affairs, though united by a common allegiance to the Crown, and freely associated as members of the British Commonwealth of Nations."

Newfoundland have voluntarily decided to leave the conduct of the greater part of their external affairs in the hands of His Majesty's Government in the United Kingdom, ... [a point] made clear by the Prime Minister of Newfoundland during the Imperial Conference of 1926 ..."[245] Newfoundland was the only Dominion that was not a separate member of the League of Nations, and that, "in consequence[,] the representation of her interests in League matters falls to His Majesty's Government in the United Kingdom, but she is fully consulted whenever those interests are likely to be affected."[246]

In June 1932, when his government was sworn in, Alderdice took on the role of Secretary of State for External Affairs,[247] along with the duties of prime minister and minister of Finance and Customs. Generally, his correspondence with Dominions colleagues was perfunctory—he sent a list of his new Cabinet ministers to the governments at Pretoria and Wellington, New Zealand; he received notice from Rhodesia about visa fees to be levied on passengers from the US. One exception to this exchange of routine correspondence was a request from Alderdice to N.C. Havenga, the finance minister in the Union of South Africa, to explore trade opportunities. Alderdice wanted to export "wooden shooks," parts that could be assembled into boxes that South African farmers could use to ship fruit. There was a strong intimation that, if such a deal could be reached, "it might be possible to come to some arrangement [to] direct some trade in [South Africa's] direction,

245 William Gilmore, *Newfoundland and Dominion Status: The External Affairs Competence and International Law Status of Newfoundland, 1855–1934* (Toronto: Carswell Legal Publications, 1988), 138–39.

246 Ibid., 139.

247 Established in 1931; prior to this time, the position was that of Colonial Secretary.

particularly in certain items, the import of which is controlled by a government department." As there were no other details, one wonders what Alderdice had in mind.

Alderdice's richest correspondence, not surprisingly, was with the government of Canada, specifically with Prime Minister Bennett and some of Bennett's ministers. These letters reveal concern about bilateral issues such as trade deals and suspected criminal activity, agitation over the deportation of Newfoundlanders, and requests for help in overhauling Newfoundland's customs duties. One letter detailed a dramatic encounter on June 5, 1933, in the Bay of Islands, involving the customs inspector at Corner Brook and the 26-ton *Marion Rita*, a vessel Newfoundland suspected of running rum from St. Pierre. The encounter gave rise to a sustained series of letters and telegrams to the Canadian Secretary of State for External Affairs. The incident began when the customs inspector from Corner Brook attempted to board the "rum runner" from St. Pierre. The report passed through the deputy minister of Customs in St. John's, who wrote Alderdice with the details, including the accusation that the "crew of [the] schooner armed with guns and other unlawful weapons, refused us to board her ..." The government at St. John's asked its customs boat at Port aux Basques "to proceed immediately to Bay of Islands with instructions to capture the *Marion Rita*."[248]

The Bay of Islands incident had international implications. Two days after the initial alarm, the deputy minister again wrote Alderdice, telling him that the schooner was registered to Enoch Tobin from Lunenberg, Nova Scotia. "May I suggest you take this matter up with the Canadian authorities," he wrote, "as it is a rather

---

248 The Rooms Provincial Archives of Newfoundland and Labrador,
    GN/8.246, Letter, Deputy Minister of Customs to Alderdice, June 5, 1933.

serious condition of affairs when a rum-runner is caught in the act of smuggling on our shores contrary to our laws." Not only that, the *Marion Rita* crew "flaunt[ed] our customs officials and the further possibility of endangering their lives."[249]

It was not until three weeks later, on June 28, 1933, that the deputy had a draft letter ready for Alderdice to approve and send to the Minister of External Affairs in Ottawa. Alderdice sent it the next day, citing the relevant section of the Customs Act for "hovering in territorial waters [and the penalty of] confiscation of vessel and cargo. I would be very grateful if you would investigate this case with a view of having the responsible parties brought to Justice."[250] But Ottawa was unwilling to get involved. In his reply to Alderdice on July 14, the acting Secretary of State for External Affairs said that he had asked the Department of Marine to act, but "it is very doubtful whether anything can be done to have the responsible parties brought to justice in Canada." Canada was revising its shipping law, he wrote, and it was "unaware [of any rule of law] that would justify proceedings arising out of this incident."[251]

Immigration was another source of tension between the two countries. Alderdice wrote directly to Bennett after Newfoundland officials raised concerns about individuals who had been deported to Newfoundland from Canada. Alderdice's first letter on November 22, 1932, included cases that officials in St. John's had culled from their files since 1927.

Three weeks later, Canada's acting minister of Immigration and Colonization contacted the Newfoundland authorities to

---

249 Ibid., June 7, 1933.

250 Ibid., GN/8.242, Letter, Alderdice to Canadian Minister of External Affairs, June 29, 1933.

251 Ibid., Letter, Acting Secretary of State for External Affairs to Alderdice, July 14, 1933.

inquire about "the full details." Newfoundland's deputy minister of Justice Brian Dunfield wrote Alderdice on January 7, 1933, with particulars: "one man back [in Newfoundland] because of perjury and venereal disease in the United States" (Canada refused to take the man back from American authorities); a second case involved a woman who had two illegitimate children. Alderdice sent these examples to Ottawa. The tone of the correspondence, which had been mostly civil, changed with an unapologetic letter from the acting minister in Ottawa, W.A. Gordon:

> in four instances the persons involved had criminal records; were not in possession of Canadian domicile, and therefore, definitely prohibited from admission to Canada under Canadian law. It has been necessary ... to strictly enforce the provisions of our Immigration Act ... there has been no discrimination of any kind with regard to citizens of Newfoundland.[252]

Alderdice's reply was critical of Gordon's account of events. For good measure, he noted, "I am forwarding a copy of your comment of the 11th of February, and also of this reply to the Right Honourable the Prime Minister":

> Your reply does not seem to me to meet the point which was made to you. Our argument is that it is not fair or neighbourly for Canada to accept whole families, including infants, retain the many good citizens among them, and select and send back to us, or through the United States force back on us, those who had turned out badly

---

252 Ibid., Letter, W.A. Gordon to Alderdice, February 11, 1933.

after they had reached adult age. The whole question is not what your present law is, but whether, as a matter of fair play, that law should be carried out against Newfoundland in cases such as those noted.[253]

Alderdice's letters in relation to this incident reveal elements of nationalism, and his sense that Newfoundland, while financially destitute, operated on the same constitutional footing as Canada. In his appeal to Bennett, Alderdice argued that the deportations to Newfoundland "constitute a distinct hardship when applied to British subjects, and is particularly severe in view of the friendly relations ... which have prevailed between our two countries."[254] Bennett replied six days later, addressing Alderdice as "My dear Prime Minister." A kind greeting—but no concession followed. Bennett's letter showed no desire to overrule his acting minister. "I will confer with the Acting Minister of Immigration," Bennett wrote, "and advise you in due course."[255]

Some of the correspondence between Alderdice and the Canadians appears to be missing from the archives, but it can be inferred that Alderdice suggested that Newfoundland might refuse to accept a person deported from Canada. "I note your reference to the possibility of refusing to receive a direct deportation from Canada," Gordon wrote on June 5, "and I trust you will not find it necessary to take such action." If Newfoundland followed through, he continued, "that would, of course, immediately necessitate the Government of Canada giving consideration to the necessity of

---

253 Ibid., Letter, Alderdice to W.A. Gordon, March 9, 1933.

254 Ibid., Letter, Alderdice to Canadian Prime Minister R.B. Bennett, March 9, 1933.

255 Ibid., Letter, Bennett to Alderdice, March 15, 1933.

prohibiting the admission to Canada of immigrants from Newfoundland."[256] Neither side would back down from its position; the letters on the immigration disagreement ceased.

The steamship service on the Cabot Strait and its connection with the Canadian National Railway in North Sydney was yet another source of disagreement between the two countries. Alderdice felt that the 20,000 passengers who crossed the Strait each year and then took the Canadian railway, as well as the annual 30,000 tons of freight to and from Newfoundland, obliged the Canadian government to contribute to the cost of this service. It had in the past: prior to 1913 Canada provided an annual $35,000 payment to the Reids, who operated the steamship service. That payment was increased to $75,000 in 1913 when a second vessel, the *Bruce*, was added. The service was reduced to one vessel in 1920 and the $35,000 annual subsidy reinstated and paid until the winter of 1924. On February 13, 1924, however, Ottawa demanded a $10,000 annual reduction in the subsidy. Newfoundland refused, and the Canadians cut the subsidy entirely 15 days later. They had paid nothing from 1924 until Alderdice brought the matter up with Trade and Commerce Minister H.M. Stevens at the Imperial Conference in August 1932.

Alderdice expected to hear from Stevens after the Conference, but by early October he still had heard nothing. He launched into a scathing attack on the Canadian position. Newfoundland was demanding "as a bare matter of justice" payments of $297,000 in arrears, "an undertaking … that there will be paid to us annually the sum of $35,000 by way of a subsidy," and half the annual cost of the operation of the railway terminal Newfoundland had built at North Sydney. Alderdice estimated it had cost $649,000 to

---

256 Ibid., Letter, W.A. Gordon to Alderdice, June 5, 1933.

operate the terminal in the years since Canada suspended payments. He also accused the Canadian railway of charging a "discriminatory rate" on freight shipped to North Sydney and bound for Newfoundland. If Canada would not address the Newfoundland concerns, "the Railway Commission is seriously contemplating running their steamers to some American-South coast shipping point that would give us the lowest freight cost for western products such as pork, beef, flour, etc."[257]

Newfoundland, of course, could not afford poor relations with Canada, considering the state of its finances, and the uncertainty of finding new loans to pay the twice-yearly interest on the debt. Bennett had helped secure loans from Canadian banks to pay the interest due on December 31, 1931, and he would be called on again a year later to assist in the payment due on December 31, 1932. As well, in mid-October 1932, Alderdice wrote E.N. Rhodes, the finance minister in Ottawa, "for help in revising Customs Tariff." He told Rhodes that he wanted a customs official "well-versed in the act of tariff making." Ottawa promised almost immediately "to do so if at all possible." A week before Christmas, with arrangements made to send two Newfoundland officials to Ottawa, Rhodes showed some empathy: "May I say how much we sympathize with you [Alderdice] in the difficulties which are facing you? My hope is that you may be able to place your financial house in order."

During this time, Canadian mining speculators developed an interest in Labrador iron ore deposits. Alderdice wrote the Canadian Secretary of State for External Affairs to obtain clearance for use of the inbound port of Sept-Îles, Quebec, as a customs post. Newfoundland would establish its customs post at a lake in

---

257 Ibid., Letter, Alderdice to H.M. Stevens, October 8, 1932.

Labrador. "This would enable the two ports to check their records," Alderdice wrote, "and make sure that neither your customs nor ours is evaded."[258]

Alderdice was also well aware that Canada was pursuing various commercial agreements with other nations, including the US and France. He was especially interested in Canadian Press reports in April 1933 that Canada and the US were negotiating a trade treaty. In his letter to Bennett, he said, "I should be glad if it could be arranged that Newfoundland be included, at least to whatever extent we might be able to participate, in a policy of reciprocal trade." Alderdice reminded Bennett of Canada's role in killing Sir Robert Bond's draft reciprocity treaty with the US in 1890, after "Canada protested so strongly to the Imperial Government."

Alderdice was similarly motivated to express his views to Canadians when he heard that Quebec was hoping to negotiate a trade agreement with Italy in order to improve markets for salt cod from the Gaspe. "I have no doubt," Alderdice wrote to the Secretary of State for External Affairs, that Canada would give Newfoundland "an opportunity of expressing [its] views in connection with any negotiations that may be contemplated with the Government of Italy, as that country is an important market for Newfoundland codfish."

Newfoundland's "independent personality" was expected and assumed in London, certainly when it involved a foreign country's request. One such instance was outlined in a letter from J.H. Thomas at the Dominions Office to Alderdice on December 19, 1932. The Italian air force planned to fly military hydroplanes from Ortobello in Italy to Harbour Grace during the next summer.

---

258 Ibid., Letter, Alderdice to Secretary of State for External Affairs, Ottawa, April 10, 1933.

"It has to be pointed out to the Italian charge d'Affairs," wrote Thomas, "that the permission of His Majesty's Government in Newfoundland will be required as regards the proposed flight to Harbour Grace."[259]

Alderdice took a more expansive view of Newfoundland's economic potential during and after the 1932 Imperial Conference in Ottawa. Rubbing shoulders with the Empire's top politicians agreed with him, as he recorded in a cable to Winter: "Coming week crucial from Conference standpoint ... putting up hard fight for increased tonnage Wabana ore. Meeting international representatives here this week. Canadians most sympathetic." Alderdice lobbied the Canadians and British to import Newfoundland cod liver oil, one item given Imperial tariff protection during the Conference. He argued not just for tariff protection in the UK but also guaranteed access, asking Britain to guarantee imports of not fewer than 150,000 gallons of cod liver oil a year.[260] Alderdice also peddled cod liver oil to the Canadians, telling them about its availability in 1- and 5-gallon tins. They provided the names and addresses of eight companies "who may be interested in obtaining supplies" and passed this information to its own Department of Pensions and National Health.

Alderdice also struck up a relationship with the Trade and Commerce minister from Australia and agreed to a trial shipment of three barrels of salt beef to determine if Australian beef producers could create a product that would suit the palate of Newfoundlanders. The only stipulation was that the quality be "suitable to

259 The Rooms Provincial Archives of Newfoundland and Labrador, GN/1/3/A, Letter, J.H. Thomas to Alderdice, December 19, 1932.

260 In 1931, the UK imported more than 600,000 gallons of cod liver oil, two-thirds of which came from Norway. Newfoundland sold just 10,644 gallons in the UK during that year.

our importers and at a price not greater than ... our present sources of supply. [If Australia could meet those requirements] ... we will make provision for a preference of three dollars per barrel in favour of your salted beef."[261] The salt beef trial came in the wake of a trade deal signed between Alderdice and the Australian prime minister Joseph Lyons in Ottawa on August 22, 1932. Under the agreement, a variety of Newfoundland products would receive tariff relief in Australia, including cod liver oil, pickled, chilled and canned salmon, dried cod, and canned crustaceans. Australia would benefit from lower tariffs on frozen mutton, canned fruits, raisins, brandy, and confectionary. It was not free trade, but it was freer trade, and in the atmosphere of Ottawa and the Great Depression, any investment in more trade was perceived as favourable.

---

261 The Rooms Provincial Archives of Newfoundland and Labrador, GN/8.239, Letter, Alderdice to H.S. Gullett, Australian Minister of Trade and Commerce, September 1932.

CHAPTER 9

The Home Fires Burn Bright

Fiery speeches were made, and some of them [protesters in
Carbonear] became more like savages than human beings.
— Constable Allan Dwyer, October 1932

Carbonear seemed an unlikely place for protest and demonstration in the fall of 1932, four months after voters elected Secretary of State John C. Puddester as their MHA. Puddester won the seat in Carbonear-Bay de Verde by 1,370 votes, capturing 63 per cent of all votes cast in part of the electoral sweep by Alderdice and the UNP—the "plain men of business." Yet, by early October, with another cold and depressed winter coming on, the unemployed rallied against the government's dole policies in several communities along the Conception Bay shore.

The Newfoundland Constabulary had a small station at Harbour Grace. When the hierarchy in St. John's heard of the discontent in nearby Carbonear, they dispatched one of their constables, Allan Dwyer, to collect intelligence on planned civil disobedience and advise the Constabulary if reinforcements were to be sent to the area from St. John's. Travelling undercover, Dwyer kept the purpose of his trip to as small a circle as possible. He wrote to the officer in charge at Harbour Grace: "I [do] not want to be known as a policeman while at Carbonear."

It would not take long for Dwyer to find that the most basic concern of the residents of Carbonear was the meagre government rations they were expected to live on that winter, the equivalent of 6 cents a day for dole.

The heavy demand for public relief commenced as the Great Depression began in 1931, and it became nearly impossible for the unemployed and poor to feed themselves. Dole was not paid out in cash but guaranteed by the government in St. John's as food from merchants around the country. The standard monthly ration consisted of 25 pounds of flour, 1 quart of molasses, 3¾ pounds of fatback pork, 2 pounds of beans, 1 pound of split peas, 2 pounds of cornmeal, and ¾ pound of cocoa. This allowance met only a small part of a person's nutritional needs.[262] Those relying on the dole, and the government to which they looked for help, were caught in the same economic maelstrom. The economy was in decline because of the Great Depression, making it nearly impossible to find jobs; this forced a substantial increase in the demand for able-bodied relief, even as general government revenue declined; and the government's search for new revenue included additional tariffs on many items, including basic food.

Dwyer stepped off the train in Carbonear on October 3, 1932. "Mass meetings" had already been held and "every person who

---

262 Jenny Higgins, "Great Depression—Impacts on the Working Class,"
    Newfoundland and Labrador Heritage, 2007, accessed March 8, 2014,
    http://www.heritage.nf.ca/law/depression_impacts.html.

attended were known and had to be on the Dole."[263] Alderdice later reported to the governor that the men in Carbonear wanted a return "to the Magor ration of $1.80 every three weeks" rather than the recently set rate of $1.60 a month.[264] Carbonear's police officers told Dwyer that the unemployed planned to come to the courthouse on October 6 and demand just that. On October 6, the air was tense as hundreds of men gathered and marched through Carbonear to the courthouse grounds. "The mob was heard to say 'we mean to have satisfaction today,'" Dwyer reported. He was convinced that "they appeared to be of that mind." The protesters put poles across the railway tracks and forced the engineer from the train. Their strategy involved not only taking a stand in Carbonear but also stopping the trains at Spaniard's Bay, 16 miles away.

The protesters commandeered automobiles; "the owners [were] forced to drive a delegation to Spaniard's Bay and vicinity to get the men who were getting Dole to form up and allow nothing through from St. John's." Sergeant George Bussey said that the 450 men, hailing from communities from Bristol's Hope to Perry's Cove, had phoned ahead to Tilton "to hang up all trains and cars coming from St. John's, especially if there were any police on board." The men intended to take their case to St. John's, as they had previously "tried getting in touch unsuccessfully with the government."

---

263 The Rooms Provincial Archives of Newfoundland and Labrador, GN/1/3/A, Box 152, Report, Constable Allan Dwyer to Newfoundland Constabulary, St. John's, October 1932.

264 Ibid., Letter, Alderdice to Governor, October 13, 1932. Robert B. Magor was a Montreal businessman appointed by Squires in the fall of 1931 to advise the government on reorganizing several public enterprises, including the railway, dry dock, and telegraph systems. Later, Magor was given authority for outport relief.

The tension was defused when businessman John Rorke spoke to the group outside the courthouse at 11 a.m. and "offered each man a month's rations." Dwyer reported that they accepted the offer, and dispersed at 12:20 p.m.:

> I am of the opinion that if Mr. Rorke had not made that offer it would have been very serious and very little of Carbonear would have been left the next day, as the mob had complete control of the Town and did as they pleased. It was difficult to say who was the worst, they were all of the same mind … several men spoke, advising them to all stick together, that they should have done this months ago. They had their way, and when the month's rations was gone, they were coming back and clean out the whole merchants; that the merchants were living on their money and they would bring them to the same level as themselves.[265]

The town was shaken by the events. Residents had been assaulted and windows broken in three stores. In his report, Dwyer noted that "the respectable citizens of Carbonear are alarmed … and a spirit of mob law prevails." He concluded that "the same thing is going to happen again unless the ring leaders are arrested and dealt with."[266] Dwyer attached a list of names to his report of those involved and the property that was destroyed. On November 3, nearly a month after the disturbance, 15 men were arrested in Carbonear. The next day, 10 others were arrested in Spaniard's Bay. Within days, the Spaniard's Bay men were tried before a

---

265 Ibid., Report from Constable Dwyer, Carbonear, to C.H. Hutchings,
      Inspector General of the Newfoundland Constabulary, October 8, 1932.
266 Ibid.

judge and special jury. The three-day trial heard from 12 Crown witnesses and 16 from the defence. The jury reached a decision in just 75 minutes: a guilty verdict against nine of the men, "with a strong recommendation for mercy." The tenth, George Reid, was released. Sentencing was on December 17, and all nine men were sent to the penitentiary for nine months' imprisonment with hard labour. The same day, the 15 men from Carbonear were sent to jail with an identical sentence. The recommendation for mercy was ignored by the court, but several of the men were granted clemency in early May, halfway through their sentence. Cabinet approved a request to have all but one of the Spaniard's Bay men released, and agreed that 10 of the 15 from Carbonear should be freed.

The unrest that eventually led to the autumn protests in Conception Bay had been simmering for more than a year. Public discussion about the startling shape of the country's finances began with a public meeting organized by Sir Edgar Bowring in St. John's on April 27, 1931. James Overton describes that meeting as "part of a growing campaign by the merchants and middle classes of St. John's to undermine the Squires' government."[267] A resolution that decried "the unjustifiable waste of public money" and the fear of "a possible national crisis" was debated, and concluded that there should be "an expert financial investigation into the country's fiscal affairs."[268]

During the four years in Opposition, from 1928 to 1932, the UNP frequently accused the Squires government of being wasteful and corrupt. But it was also true that Squires had actively sought to increase revenue from Newfoundlanders who could

---

267 James Overton, "Economic Crisis and the End of Democracy: Politics in Newfoundland during the Great Depression," *Labour/Le Travail* 26 (Fall 1990), 85–124.

268 Ibid.

afford to pay and reduced taxes for those who barely survived. In 1928, the Squires government reduced customs duties on several products used generally through the country, including twines and line employed in the fishing industry[269] and on necessities such as butter and clothing. On January 1, 1929, Squires had re-introduced income tax, reversing a decision made by the Monroe government in 1927. By 1932, income tax put more than $800,000 in the Treasury, or just under 10 per cent of total revenue. Squires had also replaced an uncollectible 25-cent-a-ton royalty on iron ore produced at Bell Island with the 10-cent-a-ton royalty, which DOSCO did pay,[270] adding $115,000 to the coffers in 1931.

Newfoundland's finance minister remained optimistic that the government could find a way out of the difficult financial circumstances. In his budget speech of April 22, 1931, five days before Sir Edgar Bowring held the public meeting to discuss the "waste" of public money, Cashin had referred to "a state of depression, bordering on despair" that existed in the world.[271] He had projected a revenue shortfall of just over $900,000 and provided an extra $500,000 for contingencies, "which has occurred in every fiscal year without exception." Despite the poor world economic outlook, Cashin told the legislature that Newfoundland was in a good position, "because when business improves depression will be more quickly lifted from us than from less fortunately situated countries." He also believed that Newfoundland would be able to raise new loans: "I feel assured that our next Loan will be raised at a more satisfactory figure than hitherto."

---

269 These duties protected the local Colonial Cordage Company, owned by Alderdice's uncles, the Monroes, and formerly managed by Alderdice.

270 Ten cents on each of the first 1 million tons, and 3 cents a ton on the next 500,000 tons.

271 *Proceedings*, Budget Speech, April 22, 1931, 300.

That optimism had been dashed when Squires had gone to the Canadian banks for a loan to meet the interest payments due on June 30. They first refused to lend Newfoundland the money, and it took Squires's personal intervention with Bennett to finally secure the loan. The $2 million loan carried strict conditions that the Newfoundland government was forced to accept. It agreed to a suite of oversight provisions, including asking Britain to appoint a financial advisor to investigate the country's financial structure. The Newfoundland government also consented to revise its system of customs duties, reorganize the public service, and implement a range of budgetary measures, including the establishment of a sinking fund for debt retirement.

That loan was the last that Newfoundland would raise from the Canadian banks. As Noel comments, "the last door of orthodox finance, held forcibly ajar for more than a year, had now been shut."[272] The austerities that followed raised fears about what would be next on the fiscal chopping block. While "bankers, businessmen and expert financial advisors could press for and demand drastic economies," the government could not ignore "the growing mob of the unemployed marching in the streets."[273] Desperate times were leading people to desperate acts.

St. John's was especially vulnerable. Employment in many of the city's manufacturing firms had been cut, leading to a high rate of unemployment. While the outport unemployed could fish, hunt, and grow vegetables to supplement public relief, this option was largely unavailable within the city. But, Noel writes, "in spite of hardships, public order in the city was not seriously threatened until early in February 1932." That spark of dissent was lit by

---

272 Noel, *Politics in Newfoundland*, 196.
273 Ibid., 197.

Cashin. Cashin's accusations that Squires and other members of his government were involved in corrupt practices enraged the public. Noel argues that, following the Cashin speech, "street gatherings of the unemployed, once passive, became increasingly menacing."[274] One week after Cashin's speech in the House on February 4, a mob of unemployed descended on Squires's office at the courthouse and forced their way past police. Once inside the prime minister's office, they jostled Squires. There was no further violence, but the group got immediate attention for some of their complaints about the dole, when the government promised to immediately process dole orders. The events of that early February day were "a frightening harbinger of things to come."[275]

Cashin had a good idea of what was to come in the winter of 1932. Even before his resignation on February 1, he knew revenues were down and spending was up. He also knew that it would be impossible to balance the budget in 1932, a commitment the government made the year before as a condition of the loan from Canadian banks. Even so, the government felt compelled to attempt to live up to the spirit of its agreement with the banks.

Squires became minister of finance after Cashin's resignation, and read the budget speech on March 1, 1932. In his opening statement, he remarked on the "grave crisis in our economic affairs,"[276] concluding that the budget could not be "balanced solely by reductions in expenditure and improvements in revenue without new taxation."[277] Squires unveiled cuts in civil service pay and war pensions and new customs duties on several imported goods

---

274 Ibid., 198.

275 Ibid.

276 *Proceedings*, Budget Speech, March 11, 1932, 3.

277 Ibid., 19.

and commodities that had previously been admitted free. He brought in new duties on essential items like beef, eggs, tea, and coal and said that, no matter how distasteful the new duties, it was "imperative in the general interests to do so and to call upon all classes of the community to assist the country in its present necessities." He even adopted the "reformist language" of Alderdice, saying "the idea has grown up that the Government has inexhaustible resources available for every citizen of the country."[278]

This budget speech was not just another budget speech, for Squires knew his political survival was at stake. He turned to "self-help" rhetoric, also a foundation of Alderdice's approach to public affairs. "We must all set ourselves to have increased self reliance and economic independence," Squires said, calling on churches, neighbours, local charities, and other organizations "to recognize their responsibilities toward the distressed before the Government is asked to step in." The goal was a "public service that is independent, trustworthy and trusted by the people," but he did not lay out a plan or a strategy to make it happen.[279] Squires's budget, while an exercise in controlling spending and finding new revenue, was also a political statement. He did not have much time to counter the impression that he and his government were not only corrupt but also responsible for the country's poor financial position.

When the legislature opened on March 23, 1932, the House began the debate on the tax and customs duties that had been announced in the budget. Squires described the increases in income tax without any commentary, although in his budget speech he had claimed that the tax was a work in progress, since his government

---

278 *Proceedings*, Appendix of Measures, March 1932.
279 *Proceedings*, Budget Speech, March 1, 1932, 24.

had reintroduced it two years earlier. Squires claimed that the increases in income tax would allow the government to collect additional money from those most able to pay and "counterbalance to some extent the Customs Duties" that forced everyone to pay more, including the poor.[280]

The increases hit single men the hardest, as the new tax rate was applied to the lowest level of taxable income. For example, after the changes Squires outlined on March 23, a single man who had paid $15.94 income tax on $2,000 income would have his tax bill more than tripled, to $57. On an income of $5,000, a taxpayer's bill increased from $111.56 to $228. By contrast, a married man with three children paid no taxes on an income of $2,000; on $5,000 income, his tax bill would increase from $35.06 to $119.70. In yet another sign of the desperation gripping the Squires government, the tax changes were retroactive to January 1, 1931. Incorporated Newfoundland companies also had their tax increased from 8 per cent to 12 per cent of profits.

During the debate in the House over the tax increase, Alderdice revealed his position on taxation. While the tax increase put "the burden ... on the shoulders best able to bear it, [Alderdice] saw it as a problem nonetheless."[281] Alderdice singled out the tax rate on "the $5,000 man," of whom there were likely few in Newfoundland at the time. "His tax rate is about 20 times greater than it was," Alderdice said, complaining that the tax was not being applied fairly. "If we were all paying the taxation we should be paying ... it would not come so disagreeably to the rest of us." He opposed making the tax increases retroactive, telling Squires that it was a "real hardship [to taxpayers] ... people living on a $5,000 a year

280 Ibid., 22.

281 Hiller, ed., *Debates*, March 23, 1932, 1:349.

salary, I don't believe had $1 of it left last December." Alderdice promised to move amendments to remove the retroactive aspect of the tax increases and to increase the tax on lotteries to 15 per cent, as "it is not legitimate business to begin with, and I don't know that it is having a good moral effect on the general public ..."[282]

Cashin, who sat on the sidelines after resigning from Cabinet, took an active part in the budget debate. He complained about the increase in corporate tax: "Surely goodness, you are not going to kill the goose that laid the golden egg by taxing the whole outfit to such an extent that people won't be able to carry on business." He also returned to his reasons for resigning: the continuing corruption inside the government. He laid out his own role in resurrecting income tax, "because members of the Government at that time did not care whether it was brought in or not." Cashin repeated his charge that Cabinet minister Dr. Alex Campbell had evaded income tax: "That one member of the Executive Council ignominiously and brazenly failed to make returns and now stays out when we are discussing it." He considered the attempt to retroactively apply the tax increase "an outrage" and was critical of government members who "come in here and sit silently. They won't express any opinion."[283]

These charges took place against the backdrop of Squires's budget, which would raise an additional $2,225,000 through a variety of increases, and, in the process, levy heavier taxes on many of the basic commodities. A barrel of flour was taxed an additional 50 cents, a $2 increase was imposed on barrels of beef and pork, and 2 cents a pound on butter. Additional taxes were imposed on eggs, tea, coal, and other goods.

Cashin tallied up the amounts the government would collect

282 *Proceedings*, March 23, 1932, 349–50.

283 Ibid., 351–52.

A crowd gathered in front of the Colonial Building, April 1932. *The Rooms Provincial Archives of Newfoundland and Labrador, A19-21*

from each of these commodities—"flour, $136,000; fresh meat, $29,700; beef, $95,396; pork, $46,878; butter, $8,864; coal, $46,000; tea, $15,000; oils and kerosene, $200,000." He derided his former colleagues on the government benches, charging that "the principle of the Budget is vicious, rotten, [and] it is going to destroy the trade of this country ..."[284]

Phillip J. Lewis, one of two government members for the constituency of Harbour Main, agreed that "the increase of taxation is obnoxious" but suggested that the government had no alternative. Lewis also acknowledged that a political price might have to be paid, admitting "that from a political standpoint voting for increased taxation is not a popular move, but [he also submitted] that the day [had] passed in this country when political feelings

---

284 Ibid., 332.

should rule one's course of conduct."[285]

Alderdice injected a partisan note to the debate: "to me it seems that the tariff is for the purposes to enable the Prime Minister to help his friends and penalize those who are politically opposed to him."[286] He suggested that local manufacturers—of which he was one—were ignored as potential engines for economic activity. "The clothing factories got a 5 per cent protection," Alderdice told the House, but "they did not want it … [and] the shoe factory got nothing." His own financial interest in Colonial Cordage and Imperial Tobacco "would not dare look for anything." He argued that local manufacturers could employ more people if the government increased tariffs to keep out goods that competed with those produced in Newfoundland. He called for the imposition of an emergency tariff until the end of June or the end of the year, so that local manufacturers "could keep open their factories and keep out any manufacture that could be raised locally," on the condition the local businesses did not raise their prices. Alderdice advocated extending the tariff protection to "manufacturers of boots, clothing, tobacco and even cordage." He claimed that such a policy would allow "a number of manufacturers running from 24 to 30 hours a week [to] enable them to run full time, and keep on their employees for 50 hours a week with no cost to the consumer."[287] Of course, such a strategy would also reduce competition in the Newfoundland market, since imported goods would cost more under Alderdice's scheme. It would also force an already destitute people to dig deeper in their pockets to buy locally produced goods.

March 1932 was a tense month in St. John's, but there were no

---

285 Ibid., 333.

286 Ibid., 329.

287 Ibid., March 22, 1932, 329.

disturbances. That changed on April 5. Noel claims that the contrasts between the severe budget measures and "the prime minister's own financial transactions were only too obvious";[288] the breaking point had been reached. A crowd of 10,000 gathered outside the Colonial Building, intent on having a delegation present its case to the government. When it was apparent that the delegation would not be given a meeting, people began to throw stones at the building. "Debate was drowned by the sound of breaking glass," and according to Noel "the public explosion had begun."[289] Squires managed to escape, and went into hiding.

Four months later, in July 1932, with the Alderdice government in power, St. John's was again a cauldron of discontent. Hundreds of men were unemployed and restless, and if it was the merchants who riled them up against the Squires government in the spring, some of those merchants had now themselves become targets.

Alderdice was meeting with DOSCO officials in Sydney, Nova Scotia, on July 25, on his way to the Imperial Conference in Ottawa when 900 unemployed met at the Church Lads' Brigade (CLB) Armoury demanding jobs. Specifically, they wondered whether the city would get a loan to start installing new water and sewer mains. It was a complicated dance—the city was already indebted to Warren Construction Company, the company that would do the work on the sewer and water mains. A delegation from the unemployed committee had met with Alderdice before he left for Ottawa, and while he said "nothing in the way of a big job could be undertaken" at that time, he held out at least some hope "that a loan of one hundred thousand dollars could be raised to start some employment …"[290]

---

288 Noel, *Politics in Newfoundland*, 202.

289 Ibid.

290 *Evening Telegram*, July 22, 1932.

Approval for the loan was slow in coming. The *Advocate* wrote that "upwards of 400 families [were] at the point of being evicted [and] families were starving" on their public relief ration. The meeting at the CLB ended with a call for the government to outline a plan for work, to stop the coming evictions of tenants, to restore the rate of public relief to what it was in 1931, and to fire its outside advisors, Penson, Thompson, and Magor, and to have "the salaries devoted to relief."[291]

The last week of July and the first two weeks of August 1932 brought hot days and warm, sultry nights. The daytime temperature stayed above 20 degrees for three weeks. The committee that met at the CLB resolved to take their case to the acting prime minister at his Winter Place home "to learn if he had received any answer from the bankers." On the way to Winter's house, some in the crowd "pelted rocks at two constables doing duty" near the Nickel Theatre. Farther along the road, "motor cars were held up, and one or two … struck with stones." By the time the protesters reached Rennie's Mill Road, the crowd had grown larger. As they passed over the bridge near Rennie's Mill, "some tore pickets off Feildian Grounds fence." They arrived at Winter's house to find that he was not there, so the procession, seeking an outlet for its frustration, continued toward the downtown.

The trouble started, according to the *Telegram*, when "a crowd broke loose" from the main group and was followed by about 20 police officers. The crowd marched down Prescott Street and "smashed 13 plate glass windows out of Royal Stores." Another squad of police officers arrived and dispersed the crowd before it could enter and loot the store. In the ensuing chase through Telegram Lane and up Victoria Street, "a number of police were hit

---

291 *Advocate*, July 27, 1932.

with stones, but none seriously injured."[292] Just after midnight, a group of 400 people formed, "armed with pickets, stones and pieces of iron," and made its way down Barter's Hill to Adelaide Street. Unknown to the protesters, the police, anticipating a second protest, had positioned themselves along the expected route. The protesters "unexpectedly encountered about 20 constables" and "[t]he police charged with their batons and a lively fight ensued for a minute." There were "many arrests."

Some of the protesters got away from the officers, and damaged several stores. The Little Star Store on New Gower Street was broken into; nearby M.J. O'Brien's store had its plate glass window smashed, "the culprits [getting] away with a couple of cases of oranges"; Nikoskey's fruit store was "entered and fruit taken"; Ford Basha's store, which "carri[ed] cakes, pies and pastry[,] was also looted"; Wylan's dry goods store was robbed; and Thomas Walsh's provision and feed store was also entered. The protesters threw stones and smashed "large glass windows" at the Board of Trade Building, The London, New York and Paris Association of Fashion, and Queen's Insurance Company.

The injuries inflicted on the police officers were reported in the next day's paper: "Cst. Slade was severely kicked; Cst. Bradbury was knocked down with a stick; Cst. Cross—ankle injured with a stone; Cst. John Cahill—knocked unconscious with a missile; Cst. Spracklin had his eye badly injured with a stone." The forces of the Constabulary were augmented the day after the downtown protest, when the GWVA offered to help patrol the city and quell any unrest. One hundred of the veterans were taken on as "special police" and "took up duty at various places and remained for the night."[293]

---

292 *Evening Telegram*, July 27, 1932.
293 Ibid.

From his safe perch at Government House, Governor Middleton sent a telegram marked "Secret" to the Secretary of State for Dominion Affairs in London. The government, he reported, was doing its best to end the protests and violence and co-operating with the city government "in a scheme for providing work for the unemployed." He told the secretary that "there has been a delay in funds being made available" and that the unemployed had become "impatient and dubious." Middleton had met with the acting prime minister and the Inspector General of Police and could report there had been 28 arrests but no information on "how many in the crowd had been hurt."[294]

Winter likely had an uneasy few days in St. John's as acting prime minister. Alderdice read accounts of the St. John's troubles in the mainland newspapers and told Winter the goings-on in St. John's were "very disquieting."[295] The prime minister promised that he would "speedily" arrange a trip to Montreal to have the banks finalize the details of the loan for the work in the capital, if Winter wanted him to do so. In his reply, Winter tried to dissuade Alderdice from making the trip. He did, however, give some credence to the "agitators'" claims that the banks' delay was leading to the trouble in St. John's: "Suggest telephoning banks and explaining outbreak last night due almost entirely to delay of banks in giving reply and is no evidence of lack of control by authorities." Newspaper reports "probably exaggerated" what had taken place, but, he allowed, the situation was "serious." He cabled: "outbreak due entirely to agitators' propaganda that government and banks were merely stalling."[296]

---

294 The Rooms Provincial Archives of Newfoundland and Labrador, GN/1/3/A, Telegram, Governor to Dominions Office, July 26, 1932.

295 Ibid., GN/8.244, Cable, Alderdice to Winter, July 26, 1932.

296 Ibid., Cable, Winter to Alderdice, July 26, 1932.

Alderdice, deciding a telephone call was not enough, left Ottawa by train to meet bank officials in Montreal. He found the "banks desirous [of] being helpful," and his instinct turned out to be correct. The loan was approved, but the banks wanted most of the money ($75,000) repaid in one year, which Alderdice considered unreasonable. The bottom line, though, was that despite Newfoundland's precarious financial position, a visit from Newfoundland's prime minister accomplished the goal of getting the funds released. In spite of the disagreement over the terms, the banks "agreed to let details stand over pending our return [from the Imperial Conference]."[297] Alderdice pledged that the Newfoundland government would guarantee the principal and interest, and at 5 p.m. on July 26, the government was told the banks had accepted the proposal.

The decision by the Montreal banks brought relief in other quarters. Middleton sent another "Secret" telegram to the Dominions Office on July 30. "There has been no further disturbance," he reported. "Agreements have been made with Banks for temporary accommodation which will enable work to be provided to unemployed."[298]

"Premier Active in Securing Loan," the *Daily News* declared, while the *Telegram* reported that "work will be started without delay." In the city, news spread quickly that the loan had been finalized. "The news of the banks … was circulated between five and six o'clock and this had the effect of easing matters up considerably."[299] The *Daily News* tried to marginalize the protesters who

---

297 Ibid., Cable, Alderdice to Winter, July 30, 1932.

298 Ibid., GN/1/3/A, Box 152, Telegram, Governor to Dominions Office, July 30, 1932.

299 *Evening Telegram*, July 27, 1932.

had damaged the city's shops, stores, and offices, saying that "the problem has been made a hundred times more difficult" for those negotiating with the banks. Through the paper's editorial page, the population was advised to "be sensible" as the city and Canadian banks attempted to finalize a deal that would get work under way on the city's streets. Civil protest, and particularly damage in the manner caused on the night of July 25, would harm the city: "The collateral which St. John's offers the banks is income derived from certain taxes. If the commercial life of the country is threatened by wanton damages, where will these taxes be derived?"[300] Two days after the loan agreement, after the residents of the city had settled down, four members of the St. John's unemployed committee were arrested and charged for their involvement in the riot.

---

300 *Daily News*, July 26, 1932.

CHAPTER 10

Desperate Means

We have economised and are economising,
but we must avoid starvation.
—Alderdice, telegram to Dominions Office, November 15, 1932

Alderdice probably didn't expect his first few months in government to be so challenging. He might have even assumed that Newfoundland's government would respond as readily as one of his businesses and that a good fiscal plan and disciplined political management would win both the election and the battle with the country's finances. In the budget debate in March 1932, Alderdice accused Squires's government of mismanagement: "All that is needed is the minor operation of cutting out graft, mismanagement and misgovernment ... With time and careful nourishment ... there is no fear ..."[301] But mid-October, Alderdice had grave doubts about what to do about the growing deficit for that year and, more pressingly, what to do about the half-year interest payment due on December 31.

Few government services were shielded from the scrutiny of the politicians, evidenced by cuts to the post office, the education

---

301 Hiller, ed., *Debates*, March 22, 1932, 1:324.

department, and pensions for war veterans and civil servants, and in increased customs duties. The railway, which had been losing substantial sums for years, was particularly scrutinized. Alderdice received the bad news about the railway's books for 1931-32 shortly after taking office. The service had just come through another losing year—a loss of $339,000 and a cumulative $2,260,911 in the preceding five years.

The Railway Commission attempted to find $180,000 in economies.[302] In their report to the prime minister and the Cabinet, the Commission identified $400,000 in savings, made up of $210,000 on payroll ("reductions in wages and reductions in hours of labour"); $120,000 in "reductions in train service, savings at terminals, adjustments in staff, etc."; and $70,000 "savings in purchases, supplies to stations, steamers, coal, etc." Alderdice received this report at about the same time as the Carbonear disturbances erupted. Government, already unsettled, took action to ensure that any future unrest would be met with adequate force. On October 18, Justice Minister Edward Emerson placed advertisements in the papers to recruit 150 "Special Constables to act as an auxiliary to the regular Force."[303] The government was looking for strapping young men, at least 5 feet 10 inches tall and weighing 150 pounds. Applicants were required to "have a fair education [and be in] first-class physical health." The pay was adequate for young men, considering that the dole rate was $1.60 a month. All the successful recruits would receive a $5-a-month retainer, and $1.65 a day "when on duty for services or drill and instruction."

On September 29, three weeks before the advertisements were placed, Alderdice said goodbye to John Hubert Penson,

302 *Evening Telegram*, October 18, 1932.
303 Ibid.

The *Evening Telegram* printing press, St. John's, 1929. *ASC Coll-137, 02.01.045*

who, as controller and deputy minister of finance, was the architect of many of the measures forced on the Newfoundland population in the latter months of Squires's administration and in the early months of Alderdice's administration. Penson, the government's financial advisor, had been seconded from the UK Treasury department in the deal Squires had been forced to accept as he scavenged for loans to meet the 1931 year-end debt payment. Alderdice expressed his appreciation for Penson's work and the difficult job he had faced in St. John's. "The reduction of salaries and other details incidental to a retrenchment program were a disagreeable task to have to perform," Alderdice wrote, "but Mr. Penson carried out his duties with infinite tact and discretion." Penson's replacement was UK Treasury official Everard N.R. Trentham. It fell to Trentham to help draft one of the most controversial and shocking papers of the still-young Alderdice administration.

Alderdice had been obsessed with meeting the year-end debt interest payment since coming into office. The cuts his government had made ensured that ordinary government spending did not outpace revenue. It was obvious, though, that the debt payment could not be met out of government revenue. Alderdice, who had developed his skills in private business and was well aware of the implications of taking on and honouring debt, contemplated what must have seemed a revolutionary act: partial default, which meant Newfoundland would pay just a percentage of the interest rate on its bonds. His first comment on the topic emerged in a letter to the Dominions Secretary on October 18, 1932. "We are carrying out immense economies," Alderdice began, and worried that further cuts would "bring the country to the brink of revolution and perhaps over the brink ..." He had been shaken by the events in Carbonear[304] and the rioting by the unemployed in St. John's in July. "I need not tell you," he said, introducing the subject of default, "how unhappy it makes me even to think of this step, but it may be inevitable ... I [felt I] ought to write at once and warn you of what may happen."[305]

St. John's residents, meantime, had become inured to the daily diet of news and announcements that suggested Newfoundland was no worse off than the rest of the world. Lloyd's of London reported in its annual *Register of Shipping* the impact of the Great Depression on the shipping industry. In 1930, 5 million tons of shipping capacity were idle; that increased to more than 10 million tons in 1931 and 15 million tons in 1932. Fully 20 per cent of the world's shipping tonnage was idle.[306]

---

304 He received a copy of the police report on the Conception Bay "disturbances" five days before he wrote Thomas.

305 The Rooms Provincial Archives of Newfoundland and Labrador, GN/1/3/A, Box 152, Letter, Alderdice to J.H. Thomas, October 18, 1932.

306 *Evening Telegram*, November 15, 1932.

The *Telegram*'s pages were filled with a mixture of hope and rhetoric. On the hopeful side, the paper reported on Britain and the other "great powers," and their disarmament proposals for a meeting in Geneva "to secure the peoples of the world against the horrors of another armageddon." Then there was cheerleading for people on the dole in St. Alban's and Deer Lake, who went to work on community projects in return for government assistance. "The Old Time Spirit" is how the paper reported the situation, as it applauded "the desire to give a return in work for assistance received." In the same article, the dole was renounced: its "effect has been to destroy public morale and to lead to the impression that individual effort was unnecessary ..."[307]

Times were hard too for the St. John's municipal government. The city was concerned that the Squires administration had laid claim to some of the money previously paid directly to the municipal council. In the March 14, 1932, council meeting, the mayor drew attention to legislation before the House of Assembly that would deprive the council "of many of its former sources of revenue, particularly Government Grants, lighting and sanitation." Council was also faced with the prospect of losing half of the motor taxes rebated to the city as compensation for the wear and tear on city roads, roads it was obliged to build and repair.[308] A city delegation lobbied the deputy minister of finance to reverse the cuts, and found instead that an additional cut had been proposed—the elimination of the Fire Insurance Profits' Tax. The Municipal Council concluded the cut would mean a loss of $60,000 in revenue and that it should write the government "to

---

307 Ibid., November 17, 1932.

308 City of St. John's Archives, City Council Minutes, 8 p.m. meeting, March 14, 1932.

reconsider its decision."[309]

As Alderdice and his ministers drafted the partial default proposal for the Dominions Secretary, the veterans of World War I launched a public campaign to lobby that the government reverse cuts to veterans' pensions. "Ex-servicemen resent and very strongly condemn the action of the government in effecting a reduction," the GWVA wrote in a lengthy letter published in the *Telegram* on October 29. That letter came out of a meeting of former servicemen at the Majestic Theatre on October 5. The government, the GWVA concluded, could find $130,000 by carefully reviewing the spending in other departments rather than by reducing veterans' pensions. It said $60,000 could be saved by "discharging extra police taken on in April and recently" and replacing the policy with "a body of 100 or more ex-Servicemen to be called out in an emergency." Another $17,000 could be saved by consolidating liquor stores and other government offices, and by more efficient use of government-owned space. It questioned the $10,000 paid to lawyers in private practice to prosecute cases when, instead, the work could be undertaken by the minister and deputy minister of justice. The GWVA's list of suggestions included combining the departments of Agriculture and Marine and Fisheries, closing the High Commissioners Office in London, and ending the practice of "certain highly paid government officials" getting "free houses, farming grounds, motor cars, fees, free light, heat, telephone service."[310]

"No substantial revenue can be raised by fresh taxation," Percy Thompson wrote, as previous budget cuts hurt buying power, cutting into Newfoundland's main source of revenue, customs duties. "There is no alternative but to have recourse to

---

309 Ibid., 10 p.m. meeting, April 21, 1932.
310 *Evening Telegram*, October 29, 1932.

further borrowing" in Newfoundland, he concluded, since Canadian banks refused to lend more funds. Thompson, concerned that Alderdice was not doing enough to cut government costs, criticized the prime minister's decision to enlarge Cabinet to 12 members. Thompson regarded the increased size as "a retrograde step; a reduction, not an increase in the number of Ministers is called for." Only four of the Cabinet ministers should receive a salary, he said, and two of those salaries should come from the payments they received for serving as directors of the International Paper and Power Company in Corner Brook: "The trappings of Government should be brought into scale with the size and economic circumstances of the population to be governed."[311]

"Secret" Telegram No. 71 was sent at 6:30 p.m. on November 15, 1932, from Alderdice through Middleton to the Secretary of State for Dominion Affairs in London. It was just 45 days to the next installment on Newfoundland's debt, and Alderdice stated that even with "immense economies [the] reverse continues to decline partly on that account, and it appears inevitable to make default, if only partial ..." He outlined what he meant by partial default: Newfoundland would pay one-quarter of the interest due on its bonds for the next four years "and various increasing percentages for succeeding years, arriving at full services, say, twenty-five years hence."[312]

Alderdice tried to anticipate Thomas's reaction. Yes, he was proposing to default on their loan payments, but, he told Thomas, but "it is only partial default." Alderdice believed bondholders would look favourably on the proposal because of the "evidence

---

311 Government of Newfoundland, Report by Sir Percy Thompson on the Financial Circumstances of Newfoundland, October 1932.

312 The Rooms Provincial Archives of Newfoundland and Labrador, GN/1/3/A, Box 152, "Secret" Telegram No. 71, Alderdice to J.H. Thomas, November 15, 1932.

of good intentions supported by degree of effort." The British would still be involved, as he contemplated "strict Treasury control" from the UK. Newfoundland had gone as far as it could in paring government spending, "but [it] must avoid starvation." The letter was sent "after deep thought" and with the approval of Trentham and Stavert.

Alderdice, the conservative politician, schooled in the art of business, less than six months into his term as prime minister, had admitted that Newfoundland could not afford to honour its debt commitments. If his proposal met approval in London, Newfoundland would pay just $1.25 million in debt charges for each of the next four years, or $5 million in total, rather than the $20 million it was facing. Had Alderdice hoped that Britain would agree? Certainly as a businessman, he would have been aware of the implications, real and potential, of defaulting on financial commitments. Or was the letter a desperate attempt to secure a lifeline from Britain, no matter the cost?

The answer came two days after Alderdice's proposal was sent. "We are greatly disturbed by your telegram," Thomas began. "We cannot too strongly emphasize our view that the action proposed would be regarded as unacceptable by holders of debt in the United States, Canada, and the United Kingdom, and our opinion is confirmed by the Bank of England." Newfoundland's proposal, Thomas wrote, "would damage credit in all parts of the Empire." Thomas did leave open the door for a partial default, with a promise to make up the difference as circumstances permitted. He wrote, "good faith requires that Newfoundland should make and continue to make to everyone the maximum payment its financial resources actually permit ... and indicating its intent to pay arrears when practicable." He suggested that, if a decision had to be made to pay some bondholders and not others, "there may be a question of external bondholders being given priority in date of payment over bondholders living within the actual jurisdiction of Newfoundland." Finally, Thomas asked if the government in St. John's had consulted Canada.[313]

Alderdice replied to Thomas at once, stating that it would be "quite impossible to pay interest and principal in full." It would also be no use to prioritize bondholders, since Newfoundland holders made up less than 5 per cent of the total: "No useful purpose would be served by consulting [the] Canadian Government." Alderdice told Thomas he did not contemplate an announcement of the partial default until about December 15.[314]

Alderdice's letters were being channelled through the Governor's Office in St. John's, and, as the correspondence carried on, Middleton began communicating directly with London on the issue. Middleton wrote Thomas on November 19 to report that Alderdice's Cabinet was solid on the partial default proposal: "The PM informed me that Ministers had expressed their confidence in him." Middleton strongly insinuated that he had told Alderdice to give up the idea of partial default: "When I saw the first message for the Secretary of State brought to me by Trentham, I sent for the Prime Minister and told him plainly what I thought of it."[315]

It took eight days for Thomas to draft and send a reply to Alderdice. Dated November 26, the letter carried a strong rebuke of the Newfoundland proposal, cloaked in threatening language. "We fear that you cannot have appreciated [the] full consequences of your proposed action," Thomas wrote, adding that the "scheme proposed ... involves direct violation of terms on which money

313 Ibid., Telegram, Thomas to Alderdice, November 17, 1932.

314 Ibid., Telegram, Alderdice to Thomas, November 17, 1932.

315 Ibid., Telegram, Governor to Thomas, November 19, 1932.

was lent to Newfoundland." He raised the prospect of Newfoundland's being blacklisted on the bond markets: "Indeed your scheme would render it impossible for Newfoundland to borrow again for many years to come in New York or London ..." Thomas saved his best argument for last in order to appeal to Alderdice, whom he knew was an avid and loyal supporter of the British Empire. "It would be not too much to say that if your scheme was adopted," Thomas wrote, "credit of every part of the British Commonwealth might suffer with risk of serious repercussions on financial and economic relations of [the] whole world." His concluding line read more like an order to Newfoundland than an appeal: "We earnestly hope that you will revise your proposal accordingly."[316]

Thomas's strident reproach put Alderdice on the defensive. The prime minister was anxious to communicate directly with the Dominions Office, rather than have his letters read by Middleton before being transmitted. On November 30, he asked Middleton to "have [the] enclosed telegram transmitted urgently to the Secretary of State, Dominions Office." Alderdice repeated Newfoundland's position that it favoured partial default and objected to an earlier comment from Thomas that "the plan ... would leave money available for the Newfoundland Government in excess of its necessities." He asked Thomas to "suspend judgment" until he was in receipt of a package by "direct mail December 9."[317]

It was now Middleton's turn to feel marginalized. He wrote Thomas that "particulars promised to you by P[rime] M[inister] were not sent through me and I do not know what they contain. I have not had any communication with PM since ... prior to sending

---

316 Ibid., Telegram, Thomas to Alderdice, November 25, 1932.
317 Ibid., Telegram, Alderdice to Thomas, November 30, 1932.

1st telegram."[318] Alderdice's mistrust of Middleton may have begun nine months earlier when the governor, in the wake of accusations from Cashin, had not found Squires guilty of any of his charges. Or it may have been that Alderdice heard about the back-channel dealing Middleton was engaged in with Thomas. Alderdice *had* communicated directly through Middleton until mid-November. Is it possible he learned of the contents of a telegram Middleton had sent to the Dominions Office on November 22, or that the telegram was the result of a row between the prime minister and the governor?

In any event, Middleton's telegram to Thomas showed his active role in trying to dissuade Alderdice from partial default. "I pointed out to him the immediate consequences to be expected from the adoption of the course proposed," Middleton wrote. Those consequences "would be financial panic here beginning with a run against the Government Savings Bank for which the Government is guarantor ..." Middleton also said that he told Alderdice that "protests would be made against [him] by bondholders against a policy never before applied by any Government under the Crown; and that Canada was interested ..." Alderdice may have already written off Middleton as a useful go-between with the Dominions Office. Middleton as much as admitted that in the conclusion of his telegram—"Mr. Alderdice said he thought I took too serious a view of possible consequences, that ... personally he felt not only hopeful but confident that in the long term, the Bondholders would come out without any loss."[319] Middleton suggested his superiors in London could help Newfoundland in other ways, without resorting to partial default. He

318 Ibid., Telegram, Governor to Thomas, November 30, 1932.
319 Ibid., November 22, 1932.

mentioned a British government loan to help Newfoundland with its interest, secured by a lien on various Newfoundland revenues, "although it might involve a restraint of Legislative powers." He blamed the new financial advisor, Sir William Stavert, for Alderdice's partial default proposal: "it was therefore not a little surprising to me to see that in his reply, Mr. Alderdice showed an unwavering adherence to Sir William Stavert's scheme."[320]

No one doubted that Newfoundland was in trouble. It was the remedy that had enraged and, finally, engaged the British. Their strategy was to get Canada involved, but Bennett was not interested. "My colleagues do not now favourably consider the idea of assistance,"[321] he wrote to Thomas on November 21. Thomas did not give up. Three days later he wrote Bennett again, noting, "we are not prepared to meet Newfoundland's obligations by ourselves and without considerations." Thomas suggested that Britain and Canada each lend Newfoundland half the amount it needed to make the December 31 interest payment and, in return, accept "a Mixed Commission of United Kingdom, Canadian and Newfoundland personnel to examine into the future of the Dominion ..."[322] Bennett was eventually convinced to participate in finding a solution. Two things had become evident: Newfoundland would not be allowed to default, and its future form of government might involve "some form of non-Responsible Government."

UK officials continued to pressure Alderdice's government to strictly control spending. Thomas wrote to Trentham, the UK Treasury official on loan to Newfoundland, on December 10, 1932, demanding to know why the extra spending of $100,000 for education and $170,000 for public relief arrears "cannot be spread

---

320 Ibid.
321 Noel, *Politics in Newfoundland*, 208.
322 Ibid.

over a longer period."[323] Trentham replied by telegram three days later in exasperation: "Treasury do not appear to realize immense volume of arrears accounts and extent to which they are now being postponed and spread," he began, noting the government was behind in its accounts by $1.1 million, including $475,000 for able-bodied relief. "These debts," he continued, "are being liquidated as and when possible, but in present circumstances this can only be done slowly, and Government subjected to unremitting and embarrassing pressure by creditors."[324]

The final details of the British-Canadian offer were settled in London on December 15, 1932, when Bennett met with the Chancellor of the Exchequer, Neville Chamberlain. Bennett came away from the meeting "convinced that Newfoundland would have to be supported." A day later, Canada and Britain formally decided to offer Newfoundland a loan of $1.25 million on the condition that Newfoundland accept a Commission to inquire into its affairs. The details of the offer were conveyed in a "secret" telegram from Thomas to Alderdice, received in St. John's at 8:30 p.m. on December 20. Canada and Newfoundland would each provide a loan for $625,000 to allow Newfoundland to meet the debt payments, and Newfoundland would provide the remaining $1,232,000. Thomas asked for a reply "with least possible delay": "In the event of your being unable to give assurance in the above sense," he threatened, "we should have no alternative but to make our position clear by public statement to the effect that financial assistance had been offered ... and had been refused by Newfoundland."[325]

---

323 The Rooms Provincial Archives of Newfoundland and Labrador, GN/1/3/A, Box 152, Telegram, Thomas to Trentham, December 10, 1932.

324 Ibid., Telegram, Trentham to Thomas, December 13, 1932.

325 Ibid., Telegram, Thomas to Alderdice, December 20, 1932.

Alderdice and the Cabinet accepted the offer. The reply was sent a little more than 24 hours later, at midnight on December 21. "We accept proposals made and are grateful for the spirit of mutual cooperation shown," it read. Alderdice also accepted the offer of a Commission made up of three commissioners: one appointed by the UK, one by Canada, and one by Newfoundland. Interest payments on the "lifeline" loan would be secured by the $300,000 annual payment Imperial Oil made to Newfoundland in return for a monopoly on oil sales in the Dominion. Newfoundland also agreed to "not alienate any substantial asset by sale or long lease without prior consultation," likely a reference to the often-expressed desire to sell or lease Labrador.

A relieved Thomas replied to Alderdice the next day at 7 p.m.: "We are glad you accept offer conveyed in my telegram." He suggested that their announcement would be delayed "until after Christmas holidays, probably December 29, and shall be glad if you would do likewise." Alderdice agreed, and nominated the financial advisor Stavert as Newfoundland's representative on the Commission.[326] Everyone in official circles in Newfoundland felt more at ease when it became known that the debt payment would be made. As Middleton wrote in a letter to the Dominions Office on December 29, "May I assure you that the splendid support given us in the matter of our debt interest far surpasses anything we dared to hope," the letter began. "It comes as a most welcome relief to bondholders and saves the country's credit and reputation from being forfeited."[327]

Britain may have preferred to keep the details of the loan secret until December 29, but the *Montreal Star* published a story, a week early, about a deal reached in London that had Britain and Canada lending $1.5 million—$250,000 more than had actually

---

326 Ibid., Telegram, Alderdice to Thomas, December 22, 1932.
327 Ibid., Governor to Harding, December 29, 1932.

been agreed on. Interviewed by reporters in St. John's, Alderdice confirmed the substance of the *Star* story by saying that "a proposition somewhat on the lines of *The Star* account but differing in the details" had been made. The *Telegram* noted that the proposal would be debated by Cabinet on the night of December 22. No mention was made of a Commission, but the *Telegram* editorial writer was comforted by "the accommodation" worked out in London. "That in itself is sufficient to enable all of us to spend the Christmas season with easier minds."[328]

Alderdice released the details in St. John's during a speech to Rotary on December 29, just as statements were being announced in Ottawa and London. The *Daily News* reported "a very large attendance" of the business leaders of St. John's—"the cream of the commercial body of Newfoundland"—for the speech at the Newfoundland Hotel. Alderdice thanked the Canadian banks, the Canadian prime minister, and the Dominions Office. He revealed some of the substance of the exchanges with the Dominions Office the previous fall, and alluded to the threat to pursue partial default on Newfoundland's debt. The tale was told in diplomatic language: "I pointed out in a letter to Mr. Thomas the seriousness of the situation in which we were placed. It was so important to Mr. Thomas that he cabled back, and distressed as he was … he said, 'you must not default.'" Alderdice made no mention of his proposal for partial default, or of the strong language and threats Thomas had used to denounce Newfoundland's proposal. Nor did he discuss his own distrust of Middleton. The deal was done, as Alderdice had proclaimed to the Rotary, and "the nightmare of default is removed for all time."[329]

---

328 *Evening Telegram*, December 23, 1932.
329 Ibid., December 30, 1932.

Alderdice was anxious to calm fears that the loan agreement, and the Commission appointed to inquire into Newfoundland's future, might lead Newfoundland into union with Canada. "We have heard a lot of talk of 'this means Confederation; we have compromised ourselves by accepting financial assistance from Canada,'" he said, but "there was no string whatsoever attached to this loan … there is no such embarrassment."

As Newfoundland's loan agreements were made in the fall of 1932, Britain was well into its own plan to shed billions in war debt owed to the US, details of which emerged from British Cabinet documents in the fall of 1931 and winter of 1932. The documents "to be kept under lock and key" described British proposals for reducing debt and suspending payments.[330] The British were sensitive about the plan, especially how it would be received by the US Congress, and adamant that nothing be said publicly about a meeting between Ambassador Sir Ronald Lindsay and president-elect Franklin Roosevelt on February 20, 1933. Several options for addressing the war debt were discussed, including scaling back payments on more than $4 billion owed to the US, waiving interest altogether, or adopting terms such as those negotiated with Italy, which carried a low interest rate. The British prime minister was so concerned about Cabinet leaks that discussion papers were collected from ministers at the end of the February 13, 1933, meeting, and the Cabinet secretary "took steps to recover papers from absent Ministers."[331] Lips were to be kept sealed until the British gleaned that Roosevelt was willing to consider a satisfactory debt repayment scheme; otherwise, it would

---

330 The National Archives, UK, Cabinet memorandum from Neville Chamberlain, Chancellor of the Exchequer, Cabinet Papers 315 (31), December 11, 1931, and 416 (32), December 1, 1932.

331 Ibid., Cabinet Meeting on The British War Debt to the United States of America, Cabinet Paper 8 (33), February 13, 1933.

be useless to have the prime minister or a senior minister travel to Washington for a follow-up visit. In the words of the Cabinet paper: "Neither Mr. Roosevelt not His Majesty's Government must be let down over the excursion."[332]

Would it have made any difference to Alderdice's negotiations with Britain had he known about the war debt proposal? It certainly would have cast Newfoundland's far more modest proposal for partial default in a different light. And it would have provided Alderdice with some ammunition in his battle with the Dominions Office to fight back against the suggestion that no Imperial government had ever defaulted on its debt obligations.

---

332 Ibid., Memoranda for Instructions to His Majesty's Ambassador at Washington, D.C., Cabinet Paper 8 (33), February 13, 1933.

CHAPTER 11

Capitulation

Lord Amulree proposes to return to the Island on
8th September in order to draft his Report, and it is
essential that he should be acquainted with the views of
His Majesty's Government before he sails.
—Neville Chamberlain, August 21, 1933

Once Alderdice had agreed to a Royal Commission, many matters were out of the control of the Newfoundland prime minister and his Cabinet. They still governed, and the legislature in St. John's continued to meet, but there was a strong sense that everyone was playing a waiting game until Lord Amulree made his report.

Commissioners Lord Amulree, William Stavert, and Charles McGrath arrived in St. John's via Halifax at 9 a.m. on March 13. They arrived on the SS *Silvia*, a former ship of the Bowring Brothers Red Cross Line, then owned by Furness Withy and Company. They and secretary Alexander Clutterbuck were met by several officials, including a representative of the governor, John Puddester, and E.N.R. Trentham.

Amulree, who had entered British politics after time as a lawyer and a public servant, was one of the few Labour politicians to

The SS *Silvia* in St. John's Harbour, post-1928. *ASC Coll-137, 03.25.023*

join Ramsay MacDonald in the National Government, which formed in response to the Great Depression. Stavert, born and educated in Prince Edward Island, was Newfoundland's appointee. McGrath, appointed by the Canadian government, began his career as a surveyor in the Northwest Territories and became a Member of the Legislative Assembly in Alberta and MP for Medicine Hat, Alberta.

The St. John's hearings were to be held in a suite at the Newfoundland Hotel, and, according to the *Daily News*, "it is understood [that the sessions] will be largely, if not entirely, confidential in character."[333] The local papers welcomed the Commission with questionable sincerity. The *Telegram*'s "cordial welcome" admitted that "the investigation may disclose sins of omission and commission in the conduct of the Dominion's ... affairs, [but] Newfound-

---

333 *Daily News*, March 13, 1933.

landers are prepared to bear the pain of having the sores laid bare, if ... the source of the troubles may be revealed and the cure applied."[334] The *Daily News* offered a "sincere welcome" to the Commission, expressing hope "that they may uncover many of our weaknesses and point the way ... which may help resolve our financial difficulties." It invoked its own medical metaphor in warning the people of Newfoundland that, "like the advice of a doctor to their patient, their suggestions will depend on our willingness to carry them out. Prescriptions alone never affected a cure ... [and] no one expects miracles."[335]

The Commission's work officially began in the main ballroom of the Newfoundland Hotel at 3:30 p.m. on March 16. Chairs were set out for 100 invited guests, the who's who of St. John's political and judicial society, including members of the appointed Legislative Council, MHAs and their wives, and the judges of the Supreme Court and their wives. Another 200 seats were available for the public. A loudspeaker was placed at a window in the ballroom to allow the proceedings to be heard by people outside on the street. People in the ballroom stood as the commissioners, Alderdice, and Chief Justice Horwood walked to the platform at the front of the room. Alderdice and Amulree addressed the meeting.

Alderdice spoke first: "All is not well with us financially," he told the gathering, adding that he believed Newfoundland was "in many ways ... more happily situated than other countries" and "that the people generally are meeting the present difficulties with fortitude ... they are bearing their difficulties as cheerfully as possible." He asked that the Commission give Newfoundland's problems "sympathetic consideration, feeling sure of [their] appreciation of

334 *Evening Telegram*, March 13, 1933.

335 *Daily News*, March 13, 1933.

the fact that our willingness to carry out our financial obligations is bounded only by the extent of our ability to meet them."[336]

Amulree's remarks suggested that the Commission would provide the "sympathetic consideration" Alderdice was seeking. There was no indication that Newfoundlanders had any reason to do anything but embrace the Commission's work, as he said, "the future of Newfoundland is, of course, for the Government and people of Newfoundland themselves to decide, and I need hardly say that we come here with no preconceived ideas ..." The Commission's "sole object [was] to ascertain and take note of the thoughts and desires of the people ... and of the facts of the position" and to "suggest such measures as may appear ... best calculated to meet the situation." Amulree explained he would hold

Lord Amulree's Commission held its St. John's hearings in the Newfoundland Hotel. *ASC Coll-137, 02.05.001*

---

336 *Evening Telegram*, March 17, 1933.

hearings in private in order to have the "closest and most intimate contact with all sections of the community"; the Commission needed to hear views in the "freest and frankest manner" and, through private hearings, "the confidence of all those desirous of communicating their views and suggestions to us, whether verbally or in writing, will thus be respected." He entreated Newfoundlanders to meet with the Commission in the spirit in which the commissioners had taken up the work and, perhaps, "that, whatever the outcome, they will always credit us with having given our best endeavours to … the oldest Colony."[337]

As the commissioners held hearings in St. John's, several Newfoundland communities, and Ottawa, Alderdice and his government battled a worsening budget crisis. His cheery words to the St. John's Rotary Club in December 1932, while welcoming the Royal Commission, had been replaced with a sober assessment that not much good had happened in the intervening six months.

Three days before his budget speech on June 29, Alderdice told the legislature he felt confident that Amulree would "justify us in the economies we have put in place." He also acknowledged that it would be impossible to cut any deeper into public services. The prime minister also made it clear he had not given up on the possibility of restructuring Newfoundland's debt, so that interest payments could be reduced. His hope was that Amulree's report "will justify us in looking for a considerable abatement on interest on our public debt."[338]

"No improvement has become visible during the conditions which showed themselves first some years ago," Alderdice continued. "I am, however, no pessimist." He again indicated his faith in

337 Ibid.
338 *Proceedings*, June 26, 1933.

the Royal Commission's "studying thoroughly and sympathetically our local conditions and our financial and business prospects ..." The underlying hope was that the Commission would recommend "the most satisfactory solution for meeting its [Newfoundland's] present difficulties." There was no talk of what that solution might entail, nor the possibility of the loss or curtailment of responsible government. Alderdice was, however, willing to "defer the proposals of the Government for reaching a balance between revenue and expenditure [until the] Commission have come to their conclusions." The budget cutting that had begun in 1932 under Squires and accelerated under Alderdice would not continue.

In the meantime, in September 1933, the Newfoundland government received an unsolicited development proposal from an American concern, Chase and Gilbert in Boston. The firm suggested undertaking a construction and industrial program to develop natural resources, build public works ("principally highways"), and finance the program through a monopoly on goods and services already being offered by hundreds of Newfoundland businessmen, including the provision of flour, sugar, and tea. In order for it work, the Boston promoters' "Interior Development Fund" would place severe restrictions on the government, impose limits on vehicle registration and licensing fees, and place duties on such goods as flour, coal, and sugar. Chase and Gilbert proposed a 30-year right to import automobiles, oils, wheat, and sugar, duty-free.[339] Deputy Secretary of State Arthur Mews examined the proposal and, after two weeks, presented Alderdice with a point-by-point assessment and rebuttal. While he had "tried to be quite fair to the company," Mews was concerned that their plan

339 The Rooms Provincial Archives of Newfoundland and Labrador, GN/8.259, Chase and Gilbert Proposal, September 26, 1933.

was "unfair to people in business" in Newfoundland, and that every cent that went into the fund would have to "come out of the pockets of the people of Newfoundland." Mews was suspicious that the principals behind the proposal had not disclosed their names, so that "the Government might have the opportunity of investigating their bonafides."[340] The proposal was rejected.

The Amulree Commission continued its work. Although its meetings were private, it is possible to piece together some of the presentations from documents that became public in 1985 through the papers of Commissioner Charles Alexander Magrath. The papers, which are deposited in the National Archives in Ottawa, refer to submissions from organizations such as the Newfoundland Teachers Association (NTA) and the GWVA, and contextualize Alderdice's remarks to the Commission's opening session that Newfoundlanders were "bearing their difficulties as cheerfully as possible."

The education system had borne more than its share of cuts as first Squires and then Alderdice reduced spending from $1 million a year to $500,000 by 1933. The NTA reminded the Commission that the government had done little to support education, noting that "all schools and colleges, except Memorial University College [were] erected by local effort and not by the government." Many teachers had been brought "to the verge of starvation," as successive budget cuts ate into already low salaries. In 1929, the NTA submission stated, the average Newfoundland teacher earned $600 a year, compared with $1,411 in British Columbia, and $1,201 in Ontario and Manitoba. By 1933, "the average salary in Newfoundland cannot ... be much greater than $300, [and] no

---

340 Ibid., Report to Alderdice, Arthur Mews's Assessment of Proposal, October 10, 1933.

other class of public servant has suffered to as great an extent." It called for an education budget of "not less than $1,000,000."[341]

The GWVA, of which Cabinet Minister Harold Mitchell had been the first president, was scathing in its criticism of the cuts to the pensions of wounded soldiers. "If the Newfoundland Government could not provide for the payment of pensions on a scale consistent with the Scales of Payments and Allowances," the GWVA stated, "then they should not have pledged the lives and health of so large a proportion of the Country's manhood ..." It reminded the Commission that pensions were awarded "on a medical basis, not an economic one." Although the GWVA acknowledged that "upwards of 60 percent ... accepted the reduction without written protest in view of the present condition of the Country's finances ... [the GWVA wanted] restoration of full pensions."[342]

The Commission also heard from private citizens who were critical of matters ranging from the church-run education system to the expense of operating the railway. Many aired complaints that well-to-do Newfoundlanders were returning from Canada, the US, and England "wearing apparel, which on their return, is not declared" and thereby avoiding paying duty. W.J. Fitzgerald of Dominion Distributors Company alleged that the "smuggling" of clothing was costing Newfoundland $100,000 annually in customs duties.[343] Aaron Stene, a private citizen who lived on Cornwall Avenue in St. John's, complained that the railway was "costing the country too much money [and] it [had] too many officials here in St. John's who are being paid higher salaries than the

---

341 The Rooms Provincial Archives of Newfoundland and Labrador, MG/30 E82, Magrath Papers, NTA Submission to Amulree Commission.

342 Ibid., Letter, Pensions Committee of GWVA to Amulree Commission, June 1933.

343 Ibid., Magrath Papers, Letter, W.J. Fitzgerald to Amulree Commission.

earnings of the Railway warrant."[344] He suggested ending free rail travel for officials and their families. The United Church Board of Education in Moreton's Harbour advocated "an amalgamated and undenominational system of education [to eliminate] waste and inefficiency."[345]

Journalist Albert Perlin appeared before the committee on March 21, and argued for a new type of MHA for Newfoundland, not a new constitution. He pointed out the necessity of raising "the standard of membership in the House of Assembly." He felt this could be accomplished by "depriving members of the right to dictate expenditures of district allowances, to interfere with civil service appointments, and to receive [fees or salaries from work outside government] that might prejudice their vote."[346] Perlin noted that he was not recommending government by commission, but by late summer, he had come around to the idea. Historian Gene Long commented that "[Perlin's] changed view would have been all the more significant in building a perceived basis of support for the Commission's recommendations."[347]

The idea of government by commission had been publicly discussed at least since Coaker put forward the idea of an elected commission during his address to the FPU Convention in 1925. Alderdice firmly placed the idea back in the public's mind in the UNP's 1932 election manifesto, and two weeks after the Amulree Commission arrived in St. John's, a public debate on the topic was sponsored by the Llewelyn Club[348] and Literary Institute of the

344 Ibid., Letter, Aaron Stene to Amulree Commission, March 29, 1933.

345 Ibid., Letter, Rev. J.T. Clarke to Amulree Commission, April 5, 1933.

346 Ibid., Albert Perlin to Amulree Commission, March 21, 1933.

347 Gene Long, *Suspended State: Newfoundland before Canada* (St. John's: Breakwater Books, 1999), 102–103.

348 *Encyclopedia of Newfoundland and Labrador*, s.v. "Llewelyn Club." The

Methodist College.[349] It was hardly a surprise that several people mentioned commission government in their appearances before the Amulree Commission, including Alderdice and Monroe.[350] Long concludes from his analysis of testimony before the Amulree Commission that the commissioners were keen to hear opinions about Newfoundland's future constitutional status:

> ... the political direction was toward a definition of how far constitutional change could be pushed, and specifically, what were the features and perimeters of this idea of commission government? To what extent was it a viable alternative? Was it, perhaps, the only alternative? And what did the witnesses think other people were thinking? Was a referendum necessary? How would the membership of a commission government be decided? A veritable Pandora's box of constitutional options lay on the table. And the untested and nebulously defined idea of commission was a tantalizing point of entry.[351]

Private citizens and politicians in Newfoundland provided detail and context to Amulree and the other commissioners in Newfoundland, but it was the Commission's reception in Ottawa that finalized the tone and the direction of Amulree's report. The

---

Llewelyn Club was formed in December 1916 by Rev. Dr. Edgar Jones of the Church of England. Its goal was the "mental and spiritual edification of men," and it became a forum for public discussion.

349 Ibid., s.v. "Literary Institute, Methodist College." The Methodist College Literary Institute was formed in 1886 by alumni of Wesleyan Academy to debate literary topics and current events.

350 Long, *Suspended State*, 79.

351 Ibid., 92–93.

commissioners met with the Canadian prime minister on May 4, prompting Amulree to report to London that Bennett "seemed anxious to help."[352] However, two days later, Canadian finance minister, Edgar Rhodes, told Amulree he opposed Confederation with Newfoundland "as the [Newfoundlanders] would really in effect become another Ireland—not in the racial sense, but a nuisance and always grumbling and wanting something."[353]

Canada had her own problems in 1933 as the Great Depression continued and rampant unemployment gripped all parts of the country. Neary paints this picture of the Canadian capital: "There in the grim summer of 1933, a fearful government, numbed by adversity, sought not fresh commitment in relation to Newfoundland but escape from her troubles."[354]

UK politicians had also come to realize that Canada would not be part of the Newfoundland solution, at least not yet. By the middle of July, Amulree and his commissioners "concluded that the business before it had boiled down to one item": would the UK step in if Newfoundland threatened to default?[355] On July 18, four months after the Commission arrived in Newfoundland, and despite the words that had been spoken in St. John's during the opening session, Amulree, Clutterbuck, and two officials each from the UK Treasury and the Dominions Office decided that some form of British control over Newfoundland affairs would be "the best course ... until such time as the country could pay its way."[356] This implied that further financial help for Newfoundland from Britain would be tied to "a

---

352 Neary, *Newfoundland in the North Atlantic World, 1929–1949* (McGill-Queen's University Press, 1996), 20.

353 Ibid.

354 Ibid., 23.

355 Ibid., 24.

356 Ibid.

strict form of control."[357] This finding was repeated in a memorandum marked "very secret" from the Chancellor of the Exchequer to his Cabinet colleagues on August 21, 1933. "I am sorry to have to trouble my colleagues during their holiday," he began, "but a decision is urgently needed on the subject of Newfoundland."[358]

Chamberlain told his colleagues that the UK would have to stand by Newfoundland on its own, as it was "clear there is not immediate prospect of help from Canada, either in cash or by any scheme of federation or for taking over of a substantial portion of the debt in return for a sale or lease of Labrador." The possibility of "wholesale or unconcealed default by an Empire Government must be ruled out of consideration," Chamberlain told his colleagues. However, he advocated that Britain take over as Receiver after "the Government and Legislature of Newfoundland ... declare themselves bankrupt and unable to carry on ..." He proposed that the UK "accept this" and issue new bonds on Newfoundland's debt with an interest rate of 3.25 per cent, much less than the 5 to 6 per cent Newfoundland had negotiated when it placed the bonds. It was not default, strictly speaking, but Chamberlain admitted to his colleagues "that this is a scheme involving some element of default is beyond question, [and] the bondholder ... may lose some benefits which would accrue from the continued fulfillment of his contract." The financial changes would have to be accompanied by "the replacement of the present Dominion Government by some form of Crown Colony Government administered from Whitehall."

The proposals Chamberlain put before his colleagues were

---

357 Ibid., 25.

358 The National Archives, Cabinet Paper 203 (33), Proposal for Dealing with the Financial Position of Newfoundland, Treasury Chambers, August 21, 1933.

hardly surprising. Before travelling to Newfoundland, Amulree met with top UK officials, and "the Newfoundland question was canvassed in all its aspects and important understandings were reached about the future of the Royal Commission."[359] One such understanding was that the removal of democratic government in St. John's might be necessary but could only occur if it was accepted by Newfoundland, the UK, and Canada: Newfoundland's position under the Statute of Westminster was that no law made in the UK could extend to "any of the said Dominions ... otherwise than at the request and with the consent of that Dominion." Despite its close ties to the UK, and even with its reliance on the Dominions Office to practice most of its external affairs, Newfoundland was an independent country and would have to consent to any change in constitutional status.

Chamberlain's memorandum of August 21, unknown to the people or politicians in Newfoundland, spelled out the Newfoundland "scheme." He gave his Cabinet colleagues a week to consider their response and planned, barring any dissent, to "communicate the Scheme forthwith to Lord Amulree."[360] Time was running short—Newfoundland had to make its next interest payment to bondholders on December 31. Amulree had his own tight schedule—he was planning to return to Newfoundland on September 8 to begin writing his report. "The practical possibility of introducing such a scheme," Chamberlain concluded in the memorandum, "depends ... upon the willingness of the existing Government to abdicate and of the Island to accept Government by Commission." He acknowledged it would fall to Amulree and the other commis-

---

359 Neary, *Newfoundland in the North Atlantic World*, 16.

360 The National Archives, Cabinet Paper 203 (33), Proposal for Dealing with the Financial Position of Newfoundland, August 21, 1933.

sioners "to persuade Mr. Alderdice ... that it is in the interests of Newfoundland to accept the scheme with the least possible delay."

Amulree and Clutterbuck sailed from Liverpool on September 8 on the SS *Newfoundland* and arrived in St. John's on September 14. The *Daily News* editorial noted that there was "much speculation" about what the Commission would recommend. It did not reveal what those rumours were, except to conclude that they were "largely imaginary." The paper was oblivious to what had already been decided. "Nothing definite can have been decided," the editor wrote, as he surmised Amulree undoubtedly "discussed the situation with the Imperial Government [and] it is even possible a rough draft of the report has been prepared."[361] On its news pages, the paper quoted the Commission and stated that its final report would not be released until mid-October. It also reported it was not the Commission's intention "to take any fur-

The SS *Newfoundland* in St. John's Harbour, ca. 1925–1940. *ASC, Coll-137, 03.05.076*

---

361 *Daily News*, September 16, 1933.

ther evidence, but that it may be necessary to have the evidence already in, enlarged."[362]

The *Telegram* was equally unaware of the discussions in London. In apparent disregard for Alderdice's statement in the June budget that "no improvement has become visible" in Newfoundland's economic condition, the paper reported that "in certain respects the general situation has improved since the work of the Royal Commission was undertaken." It cited a "bountiful harvest of agricultural products" and acknowledged that, while the shore fishery in many places was "disappointing, the operations of the Labrador have been successful."[363]

The Royal Commission reassembled in St. John's on September 15. Less than a week later, Amulree reported to London that all three commissioners had agreed to the Chamberlain memorandum. But the Newfoundland prime minister still had to be brought onside. Amulree reported to British Prime Minister Ramsay MacDonald that Alderdice "could not even discuss matters with his own colleagues" for fear that those discussions would leak out into the general population. So fearful were both Alderdice and Amulree about what was being discussed that they held their meetings after dark at Alderdice's home on Park Place.[364] Amulree described Alderdice as "lonely," characterizing him as a businessman rather than a politician, dedicated to "sav[ing] his country from the politicians."[365]

By mid-October, Alderdice had fallen in line and agreed to what was being offered. Newfoundland would relinquish respon-

---

362 Ibid.

363 *Evening Telegram*, September 15, 1933.

364 Neary, *Newfoundland in the North Atlantic World*, 30.

365 Ibid., 30.

sible government and accept rule by an appointed body of commissioners, overseen by the governor. Alderdice's ministers would be "left in the dark until the last moment"[366] regarding the details of Amulree's report. On October 17, Amulree boarded a ship and headed back to Liverpool.

On November 21, the Commission's report was released simultaneously in St. John's, London, and Ottawa. It described Newfoundland's problems as "financial and political" and concluded that it was of little use to make financial reforms without getting at the core of the problem in Newfoundland, which was "reckless waste and extravagance ... engendered by a political system which for a generation has been abused and exploited for personal or party ends."[367] It recommended that "the country should be given a rest from party politics for a period of years ... [a plan that] affords the best means of enabling the Island to make a speedy and effective recovery from its present difficulties."[368] Newfoundland's affairs would be run by the governor and six appointed commissioners, three from Britain and three from Newfoundland.

Politics, however, was not the only source of Newfoundland's problems. Amulree described Newfoundland's main industry, the fishery, as a "destructive system." Cod sold for less than $3 a quintal in 1933. Amulree said the result was that "no margin was left to the average fisherman, who was indeed fortunate if he was able to balance accounts with the merchant ..."[369] He blamed the predicament of Newfoundland's fishery on a host of factors other than the world economy. Chiefly, he blasted the credit system

---

366 Ibid., 31.

367 *Amulree Report*, ch. XI, para. 634 (2).

368 Ibid., para. 634 (3).

369 Ibid., ch. VI, para. 274.

whereby merchants outfitted fishermen for the season in return for purchasing their fish. He also faulted the curing methods, the unwillingness of many fishermen to chase fish in the fall when cod were at their healthiest, and the practice of merchants fixing a price for all fish, regardless of the quality:

> The individual fisherman naturally asked himself why he should take trouble with his fish (and the making of a good cure calls for skill, patience and constant watchfulness) when his neighbour took none and received the same return.[370]

Such practices, Amulree said, were "largely responsible for the loss of reputation suffered by Newfoundland products in the principal markets." There was little hope for the industry, unless fish exporters took notice of their main competitors and changed their practices:

> … Norway and Iceland produce only heavy-salted fish, of the "Labrador style," and, while these have gradually ousted Labrador fish from the first place in the European markets taking heavy-salted fish, they have not so far interfered with the markets for Newfoundland's shore-fish. Seeing that the Labrador fishery has been accustomed to produce annually about 320,000 quintals and supports a considerable proportion of the population, it could hardly have been supposed that the loss of first place in the markets would have been accepted by the Newfoundland exporters with indifference. Yet, instead of being alarmed at this development and ex-

370 Ibid., para. 278.

erting themselves to recover the lost ground, the exporters have been content to explain with pride that no country in the world can compete with Newfoundland's shore-fish, which is therefore in an impregnable position. The loss of the principal markets for Labrador fish, which has involved the selling of the fish to the poorer markets at low prices, is dismissed as a temporary phase of no great consequence so long as the markets for shore-fish are retained.[371]

Amulree concluded that the main weakness of the Newfoundland fish mercantile system was its insistence on individual rather than collective action. Had the industry acted collectively firms would have been able "to weather a temporary period of depression without penalizing the actual producer, viz., the fisherman, on whom, as ever, the main burden now falls."[372] But exporters were not about to do that:

> They have insisted on conducting their businesses on a basis of pure individualism without regard to the true interests of the country and without regard to the successes achieved by their foreign competitors. Intent only on outdoing their local rivals in a scramble for immediate profits, they have failed to realise that time does not stand still.[373]

Amulree was also sharply critical of Newfoundland's public pension system. Alderdice had promised to reform the system by making it contributory, and ending the practice of dispensing

---

371 Ibid., para. 289.
372 Ibid., para. 286.
373 Ibid., para. 287.

pensions without proper actuarial assessment. But by the time he came to power in 1932 that would have been little more than dressing on a wound. The pension problem had been festering for decades. Amulree concluded that until the Alderdice government came to power, it was "quite common" for the government to ignore even the modest pension qualification thresholds:

> A Government desiring either to make room for its supporters or to reward its favourites already in the public service could introduce a Bill into the Legislative Assembly providing that pensions of specified amounts should be granted to named individuals. This Bill, when passed, was deemed to override the Pensions Act and the pensions thus granted were frequently inconsistent with the established regulations.[374]

Newfoundland's regime of tariffs and customs duties, including the calculation of duties, was also problematic. The system caused the Commission "serious concern [as] not only is there a very wide range of duties, few commodities being exempt, but the duties are in many instances so high as to be seriously oppressive."[375] It singled out increases implemented in 1932 and 1933, as first Squires and then Alderdice attempted to keep revenue up:

> Until recently it was the policy of Newfoundland Governments to admit free of duty those articles such as flour, salt and petrol which were among the essential requirements of the fishermen; to-day even these articles are taxed, and

---

374 Ibid., para. 570.
375 Ibid., ch. IV, para. 159.

the resulting increase in the fishermen's costs has proven a severe handicap to the rehabilitation of the industry in the face of foreign competition.[376]

Amulree concluded that the system of customs duties was an excessive burden on the lower classes and needed to be overhauled. He also recommended that the cuts in war pensions be at least partially restored as soon as possible and the education budget increased urgently.[377]

It is easy to find fault with a system, and it could be stated that Amulree compiled evidence to support the Commission's main conclusion that responsible government be suspended in Newfoundland. In contrast to his strong views on the fishery and customs duties, he was lukewarm on the long-running campaign to have Britain import ore from Bell Island, a conclusion that read more like a suggestion than a recommendation:

> ... if even a modest proportion of the ore imported into the United Kingdom could be taken from Newfoundland a great impetus would be given to the Bell Island Mines, with corresponding advantage to the Dominion.[378]

Even if the appetite for a drawn-out public debate about Amulree's report had existed in Newfoundland, the government in Britain was in no mood to have one. A schedule outlining how the report would be handled in the Newfoundland Assembly and at Westminster was sent through from London to the governor. The

---

376 Ibid., para. 159.
377 Ibid., ch. XI, recommendations 6, 8, and 9.
378 Ibid., ch. VII, para. 443.

report would arrive in St. John's on the SS *Newfoundland* on November 14. One week after receiving the report, Newfoundland's House of Assembly and the Legislative Council would have four days to debate and adopt its contents. A message was to be sent to the Secretary of Dominion Affairs in London on November 30 "informing him that the address has been passed in both Houses of Parliament [in Newfoundland]."[379] On December 1, the Newfoundland Bill would be introduced in the British Parliament "with a view to it being passed before Parliament adjourns for the Christmas recess."[380] The schedule was tight. No room was being left for Newfoundland's politicians to change their minds on the arrangements agreed to before Amulree returned to London.

---

379 The Rooms Provincial Archives of Newfoundland and Labrador, MG/2.16.3, "Timetable for Suspension of Responsible Government: November 1933."

380 Ibid.

CHAPTER 12

Turning Out the Lights

By the time Alderdice rose from his seat in the House of Assembly on Tuesday, November 28, 1933, any hope of retaining responsible government was lost. The Amulree Report, whose contents had been known to Alderdice since early fall, had laid the bargain on the table. Newfoundland would no longer have to search for millions to meet its twice-a-year debt payments if it closed its Assembly and gave control of its affairs to the governor and six appointed commissioners.

Liberal leader Gordon Bradley zeroed in on the implications of adopting Amulree's report and the consequent loss of a free and elected House of Assembly. "There is, Sir, an outstanding objection to these proposals," he told the House, "and that is, Sir, the strangely light and even facetious treatment that is accorded to the principle of representative government; no serious consideration is given to it at all."[381] Bradley invoked the words of Abraham Lincoln—"good government is not a substitute for self-government"—and moved several amendments, including

---

381 Hiller, ed., *Debates*, November 28, 1933, 2:512.

having Amulree's report judged by the people in a referendum or in a general election. Failing that, Bradley suggested that a three-member delegation go to London and negotiate terms "that will not involve loss by Newfoundland of representative government."

Bradley reminded Alderdice that he had made a promise in the 1932 campaign to hold a referendum on any change in Newfoundland's governance—"part of his share of the bargain," as Bradley put it. Conditions in Newfoundland might have changed, Bradley pointed out, "but [Alderdice's] promise has not changed. He cannot say that he did not know the conditions of the country at that time ... He could not have anticipated that his return to power would be followed by a general uplift in trade and that there would be work for everybody ..." Bradley laid down his markers for posterity only, acknowledging, "I am well aware of the fact that nothing that I can say will make any difference." He challenged Alderdice's assertion that the Commission of Government was "going to be for a short period" and predicted it was "going to be many years before Newfoundland [was] self-supporting again," and in the position to elect a government. "I believe my justification will come with time," he concluded.

Alderdice refused to directly address Bradley's challenge to put the Amulree Report to a referendum or an election; nor did he debate Bradley's suggestion to lead a delegation to London to demand better terms. Alderdice had clearly made up his mind: "I am afraid there is nothing for us but take it or leave it ... [Amulree's recommendations] have come to us unasked and unsought [and] the terms that have been offered are so very generous that it seems to me it would be ungracious to ask if they could be improved upon."[382]

---

382 Ibid., 506.

The right to have an elected Assembly in Newfoundland had been won 78 years before after a tough six-year battle that culminated in the general election of 1855. As Alderdice stood in the legislature and pronounced his government's support for Amulree's recommendations, he questioned the benefits of a government elected by the people of Newfoundland. "What good does this vote do for us?" he asked the members who had taken their oaths as MHAs not two years earlier. "Has it not degenerated the great bulk of our people?" Alderdice said in Newfoundland's case, "[responsible government] is only a theoretical boon and not what it is cracked up to be."[383] It was an astounding performance by Alderdice, who, two years previous, had advocated a referendum on its future form of government should the country be unable to sustain itself. A year previous, he had advocated partial default in order to keep Newfoundland afloat. Alderdice had fully capitulated, accepting Amulree's conclusion that Newfoundland's problems could not be solved without the suspension of responsible government. "Measures designed to alleviate the present burden of public indebtedness would not, in themselves, provide a solution of the Island's difficulties," Amulree had written, "since those difficulties are largely due to the reckless waste and extravagance, and to the absence of constructive and efficient administration, engendered by a political system which for a generation has been abused and exploited for personal or party ends."[384]

Alderdice had steeled himself for the possibility of change in Newfoundland back when he accepted the appointment of the Royal Commission. "[M]y colleagues and myself have had to face

---

383 Hansard (unpublished), Vol. 5, 4:15–4:30 p.m., November 28, 1933, 3. Centre for Newfoundland Studies.

384 *Amulree Report*, para. 623 (2).

this situation for some months—that we were at the end of our financial tether," he had told the Rotary on December 29, 1932. He noted that the nation was two days from "commemorating the 100th anniversary of parliamentary life in this country ... we have had one hundred years of parliamentary life, and we owe $100-million—nothing to be proud of ..."[385] He had reminisced about how the first Newfoundland assembly, comprised of 13 members representing nine districts, had met in Mrs. Travers's Hotel. When Mrs. Travers discovered that the bill was not being paid, she seized the Speaker's chair, and the hat and sword belonging to the sergeant-at-arms. The members rallied and collected the outstanding amount—£108, 6 shillings, and 6 pence. Alderdice told his St. John's business audience that "even in those days, it will be seen, our Parliament was in difficulty. We started early in the game ..."[386]

When he addressed the House on November 28, 1933, Alderdice was certain of his political footing. Several of the country's leading organizations agreed with the Amulree Report's conclusions, and the two St. John's papers, which reflected the opinions of the city's mercantile and political elite, were also firmly on the government's side.

---

385 Jeff Webb, "Representative Government, 1832–1855," Newfoundland and Labrador Heritage, accessed on July 31, 2014, http://www.heritage. nf.ca/law/representative.html. Representative government was approved by Britain for Newfoundland in 1832, and with the election of 15 representatives in 10 districts that fall, the new form of government came into effect in 1833. The new members had some power, since their agreement was necessary for legislation, including financial decisions. However, the executive held most of the power; it included the governor and people chosen from the appointed Legislative Council. Over time, the elected members pushed for greater power, and gained that status with responsible government in 1855.

386 *Evening Telegram*, December 30, 1932.

It had taken eight months from the time Amulree and the commissioners had arrived in St. John's for them to produce a report, bring about the consensus to cancel the 1855 Letters Patent which established Newfoundland's constitutional system, and replace it with new legislation to put in place an unelected government by commission.

Amulree convinced Alderdice to support the removal of a freely elected assembly in a series of private meetings help after Amulree returned to Newfoundland in early September, just weeks after Chamberlain had laid out the "Newfoundland Plan" in Westminster. It was disingenuous for Alderdice to suggest to the House on November 28 that he was surprised at the final recommendations: "I was sitting with my colleagues in the Executive Council Chamber when the Report was released. I believe the generosity of the terms nearly took our breath away."[387] The truth was, two days after Amulree returned to St. John's from London he had sent Alderdice a written copy of the offer generated by Chamberlain and approved by the British Cabinet. Shortly after, Amulree had the other two commissioners agree to the recommendations.[388]

The *Evening Telegram* and the *Daily News* began publishing the text of the Amulree Report the day after it was released. "One cannot but be impressed by the immensity of the task which Her Majesty's commissioners undertook," the *Telegram* proclaimed on its editorial page on November 22, as it complimented the commissioners on "the scrupulous care which they exercised in the gathering of the necessary information." The paper attempted to gauge the weight of the moment for the legislature, concluding

---

387 Hansard, 4:15–4:30 p.m., November 28, 1933.

388 Neary, *Newfoundland in the North Atlantic World*, 29–30.

that "it is impossible to exaggerate the gravity of the responsibility that rests upon that body." No matter how momentous the decision to give up responsible government, the *Telegram* noted that government members did not have a choice: "Will we place first political institutions which … have been declared unsound or incompetent, or will we place Newfoundland's interests first? Can there be the slightest doubt as to what the answer will be[?]" While the editorial writer "appreciate[d] the position in which the members of the Government are placed … no greater sacrifice could be asked of any group of men, and no greater test of their loyalty to country could be demanded …"[389]

The *Daily News* was equally effusive in its praise: "the proposals offer Newfoundland an opportunity for rehabilitation such as was not expected in our most hopeful dreams."[390] The loss of self-government was regarded as a fair bargain—"Newfoundland is asked in return to agree to control for a period of time by a Commission …"[391] The next day, the paper argued even more forcefully that the end of elected politics had to be viewed in the context of "the generosity of the offer" from Great Britain, and concluded, "if there was at first some opposition expressed to the temporary surrender of our parliamentary independence, it seems to have disappeared almost entirely as the nature of the proposals and the altruistic offer made to assist an overburdened section of the empire were better appreciated."[392]

The voices of opposition both inside and outside the House of Assembly were drowned out by forces in business which would not

---

389 *Evening Telegram*, November 22, 1933.

390 *Daily News*, November 22, 1933.

391 Ibid.

392 Ibid., November 23, 1933.

have to deal with the uncertainty of default and the consequences for their firms and personal wealth. Alderdice's supporters voiced no objections to Amulree's report. Instead, they made much of the fact that they were willing to sacrifice their own political dreams to save their beloved Newfoundland. That was the theme the St. John's dailies exploited and one that Alderdice carried into the legislature. "I know that some of them cherish political ambitions," he said of his colleagues in government, as he addressed the House, "but when I put the matter squarely up to my associates, they immediately agreed to make the sacrifice required in the best interests of the country ..."[393] The *Daily News* congratulated government members for taking "a patriotic stand [and they] are deserving of congratulations for their willingness to prove their readiness to forget self-interest in the best interests of the country."[394] The *Telegram*, on hearing from Alderdice that the members would unanimously back the Amulree Report, concluded that, "for their action today, they stand high in the estimate of their fellow countrymen."[395]

The sting of Amulree's report was that self-government had been so manipulated by Newfoundland politicians for their own benefit that there was no value in preserving it. That conclusion was agreeable to the elites in St. John's, including the government, businessmen, the newspapers, and the Church of England. The *Daily News* printed a sermon from Anglican clergyman Canon Stirling, who told his congregation that "this country has suffered much at the hands of political adventurers, and it is high time to put a stop to this practice." The loss of responsible government was of no consequence to the venerated clergyman:

393 Hansard, 4:00–4:15 p.m., November 28, 1933.
394 *Daily News*, November 24, 1933.
395 *Evening Telegram*, November 25, 1933.

"Fellow countrymen! Let us thank God and take courage."[396] A similar sentiment was expressed in the weekly bulletin from St. Thomas' Anglican Church on Military Road, the church Alderdice worshipped in, as it congratulated the commissioners for their work and applauded the government for implementing Amulree's recommendations: "Their names shall go down in history as those to whom we owe a debt which can never be adequately repaid."[397]

Alderdice was praised by Dr. William Blackall, a former president and vice-president of the Council of Higher Education,[398] and a man who had dedicated his life to improving education and teaching standards in Newfoundland. In a letter to Alderdice from his home at The Rectory in Annapolis Royal, Nova Scotia, three weeks after the Amulree Report was approved, Blackall was concerned about some "unhappy pension business" and that someone had suggested to the prime minister "that I [Blackall] was not entitled to consideration on the score of that 290-dollars ..." He was willing to let the matter "rest for the present [and] await the policy to be adopted by the Commission of Government ..." Blackall agreed with Alderdice that responsible government should never have happened. Britain's first mistake, Blackall said, "was in granting full responsibility to little Newfoundland." He praised Alderdice's speech in the last sitting of the House, perhaps hoping for a favourable decision on his "unhappy pension business." He wrote,

396 *Daily News*, November 27, 1933.

397 Ibid.

398 The Council of Higher Education was made up of representatives of the religious denominations which ran the Newfoundland school system. It was formed by an Act of the legislature in 1893 to promote university education for Newfoundland students in Canada, the United States, and the United Kingdom.

"indeed the peroration was in its way equal to anything that Pitt, Burke, Lincoln or Gladstone ever delivered."[399]

Former prime minister Monroe also condemned Newfoundland's experiment with responsible government. Monroe spoke from the Legislative Council and moved for the appointment of a committee to thank the governor for his Speech from the Throne that outlined Amulree's recommendations. "Responsible Government was the ideal form of government," Monroe told the Council, but not for Newfoundland, since "to us it has been a very expensive luxury." Newfoundland would have been better suited to the status of a Crown Colony run by a British-appointed governor and a locally appointed or elected council rather than a full-fledged Dominion with the right to make its own laws without reference to Britain. "[Monroe] could not help feeling," the *Daily News* reported, "that if this country had a government similar to that of Barbados or Jamaica, we would be in a very different position from what we are today." Monroe's speech admonished the very people whose government was being taken away: "Have we had it?" he asked, referring to responsible government. "If we have, surely the people cannot escape their responsibility for the present condition and deserve to have their authority curtailed."[400]

Fish merchant Daniel Ryan seconded Monroe's motion, and was equally adamant that the people of Newfoundland deserved what they were being given: "We are paying dearly for our reckless and extravagant governments of the past, [and] hoped the country had learnt a lesson that future generations would benefit by …"[401]

---

399 The Rooms Provincial Archives of Newfoundland and Labrador, MG/216.4, Letter, Dr. W.A. Blackall to Alderdice, December 23, 1933.

400 *Daily News*, November 28, 1932. Monroe expressed similar views in his appearance before the Amulree Commission.

401 Ibid.

The few who objected to Amulree's report had neither the standing in the legislature nor the social and business status in Newfoundland to make a difference—and there were not enough of them. The debate at the Board of Trade revealed that Peter Cashin and E.J. Godden, while supportive of the Commission of Government, felt that the measure should not be pushed through without the consent of the people.[402] Godden felt strongly enough about the loss of responsible government—"he thought the people ought to be consulted before giving up [their] liberty"—yet he was the only member to vote against the Board's motion to support Amulree's recommendations. The motion recorded that the organization "regrets the loss, even temporarily of the proud privileges and principles of responsible government." Still, it saw the "necessity for adoption of the proposals, involving temporary constitutional changes …" Edgar Bowring moved the Board's motion and "emphasized the wonderful generosity of Great Britain and expressed conviction we should not hesitate in accepting." Ches Crosbie, renowned in the fish business, and the father of future Newfoundland and Canadian finance minister John Crosbie, took offence at some of the criticisms levelled by Amulree, but said that "there were two choices—to accept the Commission or collapse."[403]

The loss of responsible government was seen by the political and business leaders in St. John's as acceptable collateral damage on the way to solving Newfoundland's financial problems. This position was aided largely by the two daily newspapers, themselves closely associated with those elites.

On the northeast coast of Newfoundland, the *Advocate* was skeptical, even before the Amulree Report was published. Four

---

402 Ibid., November 25, 1933.
403 Ibid.

days prior to its release, the paper noted that while "members of the Executive Council state persistently that they have no knowledge of the report [Alderdice] hinted at the opening of the Industrial Fair that we are not to expect anything handed to us on a silver salver." The *Advocate* writer continued, "the truth is, we don't expect it, but Mr. Alderdice evidently knew enough of the nature of the Report to throw out a hint to those who are not yet sufficiently disillusioned as to what might be expected from the Commission."[404] The paper called on readers to make up their own minds about the report, as "it will be up to us as Newfoundlanders to weigh well, and ponder well, the substance of the report and decide for ourselves what our reactions might be. We are yet a sovereign people, our bondholders notwithstanding."

A week later, the *Advocate* reprinted criticism from Coaker, which appeared first in the *Telegram*. "I approve of Government by Commission provided proper safeguards are afforded our people," Coaker began, but "I am absolutely opposed to the scheme as outlined in the Report." His chief concern was that the new form of government would remove all form of control from the people of Newfoundland: "Not alone does it involve the complete abrogation of our rights of self-government, but proposes to set up a governing body vested with the widest and most autocratic powers, uncontrolled and uncontrollable so far as the people of Newfoundland are concerned, who are denied even the right of selection of those to whom they are asked to surrender their liberties ..."[405] Coaker concluded that the politicians who implemented such a scheme "will be remembered in the history of this country as traitors to the land that bore them."

---

404 *Advocate*, November 17, 1933.
405 Ibid., November 24, 1933.

The *Advocate* was critical of "the indecent haste which characterized the proceedings at the Legislature"—Amulree's recommendations were introduced in the House of Assembly on Monday, November 27, and passed three days later. It accused the Alderdice government of having "taken from [the people] without their consent, their constitutional rights as Britishers to exercise their franchise in determining what type of Government we shall endure," and it was especially critical of the MHAs from the fishing districts of Twillingate and St. Barbe who had moved and seconded the Throne Speech that introduced the report. "The fishermen and toilers of these two Districts," it continued, "would no doubt like to know what reasons these two representatives had to offer for the stand they took on Monday, in joining with their leader in an act of bad faith toward the people."[406] The paper criticized Alderdice for having reneged on his "solemn undertaking" to hold a referendum should the Commission of Government be under consideration. "The people have been the victims of a huge piece of treachery," the paper concluded.

The *Advocate*'s views were not shared by the *Twillingate Sun*, which addressed Alderdice's election promise of a referendum on the Commission of Government this way: "we are under a moral obligation to immediately dissolve Parliament instead of allowing the matter to be submitted to the people under a referendum. The Country is insolvent …"[407] A week later, the *Sun* offered more skepticism: "Little do they [the people] consider how dependent we were upon the money lenders from outside the country."[408]

The FPU made two critical mistakes which took it out of the

---

406 Ibid., December 1, 1933.

407 *Twillingate Sun*, December 9, 1932.

408 Ibid., December 16, 1933.

debate about Newfoundland's political future. First: the party did not contest the 1932 election. Coaker retired from politics, and many other long-standing MHAs stepped aside, some to accept government jobs that were later cancelled by Alderdice. Second: it offered unconditional support to Alderdice's 1932 campaign promise to establish a government by commission, if Newfoundland was unable to find a way out of its financial mess. The effect of these two missteps by the FPU was to leave the political field almost entirely to Alderdice and his pro-business government, leaving virtually no one in the political establishment to fight for better terms from Britain, including a more accountable system of government in the wake of the Amulree Report. Coaker wrote a letter or two to the papers to decry the direction recommended by Amulree, and the *Advocate* challenged voters to ask campaigning politicians to outline their position on Newfoundland's constitutional future. But those questions and criticisms were coming from the outside, and in the end, were ignored by politicians. The criticism directed at Alderdice by Coaker and the *Advocate* after the adoption of the Amulree Report could just as appropriately have been directed inward at the FPU's own strategic political mistakes.

On the west coast at Curling, the *Star* adopted a tone similar to that of the St. John's dailies and expressed joy that Britain "[was] prepared to be very generous to Newfoundland." The paper noted that, "while we all deplore the suspension of our autonomy … we have gotten ourselves into a mess from which we are unable to extricate ourselves without assistance."[409] And, a few days later: "This past week has been a momentous one for this Country." The *Star* placed the blame for the failure of responsible government squarely at the feet of the people of Newfoundland: "It is not

---

409 *Western Star*, November 29, 1933.

human to desire curtailment of freedom and power, or to forego privileges enjoyed. We have had our experience, however, and we have failed."[410]

The debate in Newfoundland, in the newspapers and the House of Assembly, was short and one-sided. The House of Assembly and the Legislative Council dispensed with the Amulree Report in just a few days. In London, Parliament debated the end of responsible government in its oldest colony for several days, and on one day, December 14, 1933, the debate continued through the night until after 8 a.m. The debate at Westminster was led by politicians sympathetic to Newfoundland's cause. MPs expressed concern that, under the new Newfoundland constitution, the people would have no say in who became their government, and that the solution was entirely about ensuring that the bondholders were secure. Self-interest was also at play—would Britain get preferential treatment for its products in Newfoundland?

Chamberlain told the Commons that helping Newfoundland was a matter of duty. "It is our proud boast that up to the present time no Empire Government, indeed, I believe, no Empire municipality even, has ever yet defaulted," he said as he opened the debate on December 7, "and it would indeed be a sad and tragic thing if for the sake of a comparatively small country, ... we should allow this magnificent record to be broken in upon now."[411] Great Britain, he explained, would cover any shortfalls in the Newfoundland budget until 1936 with grants rather than loans:

---

410 Ibid., December 6, 1933.

411 House of Commons Debates, UK, December 7, 1933, para. 1850, http://hansard.millbanksystems.com/commons/1933.

> It would be rather absurd to begin the new arrangement
> by adding to the debt of Newfoundland ... we propose
> that whatever advances are necessary to make good the
> deficiencies in the Newfoundland budget shall be in the
> nature of a free gift from this country.[412]

If Newfoundland continued running deficits after 1936, Chamberlain added, that situation "can be discussed better when we know the conditions at that time."

It was up to Chamberlain's colleague, Dominions Secretary Thomas, to explain to the British House of Commons the political rationale for what Amulree had proposed for Newfoundland. "We could have frankly said to her: 'We will do nothing,'" Thomas said, adding that default for Newfoundland would have been a "disastrous" step, both for Newfoundland's future ability to borrow and for the borrowing capacity of the other dominions. "No one in this House could for one moment suggest that the repercussions which would have followed the default by Newfoundland would not have had been far more serious in their financial effect than the cost which we have undertaken in this matter." Thomas also talked about the duty Britain felt to its oldest colony as a result of Newfoundland's participation in World War I. "We are not unmindful of their obligations to this country during the War," he said. "It would be a very poor response and would show little gratitude on our part if, in their hour of need, we were unmindful of the contribution which they then made."[413]

Acting Labour leader Clement Attlee rejected the fear of default as being "a very old nineteenth century attitude, [since] all

---

412 Ibid., para. 1854.

413 Ibid., December 12, 1933, para. 222.

the best countries default nowadays … The French did not manage to pay up all that they owed, the Italians did not pay back all they borrowed in the War. Germany has not paid, and we ourselves are not paying the United States of America."[414] The real concern for the UK government, he told Thomas, "is not providing something to tide Newfoundland over their difficulty, it is providing something for the people who have lent their money to Newfoundland."[415] Junior Cabinet minister Leslie Hore-Belisha had a similar view, declaring "the primary object [of the Newfoundland Bill] is to try and keep going interest for the rentiers."[416] The majority of the bonds were held in London and New York, with a smaller amount held by the Canadian banks.[417]

As the debate in the UK parliament was in full flight, the *Telegram* lambasted the *Advocate* for its criticism of the Amulree Report. "It is impossible to believe that they are prompted by any more worthy motive than to keep the political fires burning," stated its editorial on December 12. "If it cannot rise to the occasion and play its part, … it should at least have sufficient sense to realize that it is butting against public sentiment, and keep quiet." The irony of course, is that the *Advocate* attempted to generate public debate about the report, while the St. John's papers did not raise a single objection to Amulree's recommendations. It was also noteworthy that the debate in London was not only longer than the proceedings in the Newfoundland Legislature but also included changes to the legislation. The House of Lords, concerned perhaps with the perception associated with an outright and

---

414 Ibid., para. 227/228.

415 Ibid., para. 227.

416 Ibid., para. 231.

417 *Amulree Report*, 187, 188.

open-ended revocation of self-government in Newfoundland, recommended that Newfoundland's Letters Patent be "suspended" rather than revoked, an amendment the House of Commons accepted.

In Newfoundland, the *Daily News*, which had encouraged patriotic Newfoundlanders to do the right thing and accept Amulree's recommendations without any delay or change, viewed the London amendment as one more selling point. "Those who feared the loss of Newfoundland's autonomy, perhaps forever," it stated on December 22, "can be reassured by the amendment ... [that the Letters Patent] are not cancelled, but suspended for a period of time."[418] It predicted that Newfoundlanders would "celebrate Christmas in a more hopeful and confident spirit than for some years."

On December 21, *The Newfoundland Act, 1933* was given Royal Assent by the king, and Newfoundland's 78 years of responsible government came to an end. That night, Alderdice's party fêted him with a dinner and tribute at the Newfoundland Hotel. Secretary of State Puddester, a shareholder and former business manager of the *Daily News*, chaired the evening and paid a glowing tribute to his leader. Over a dinner of boiled salmon, broiled lamb chops, and roast turkey, toasts were given to Alderdice, the king, and "our country." The UNP presented Alderdice with silver candlesticks and a silver serving tray.

Many matters remained unsettled. Who would be the Newfoundland commissioners? Would some of Alderdice's Cabinet ministers be given jobs in the new government?

In the St. John's press, the granting of Royal Assent to *The Newfoundland Act* was greeted with relief and the sense that it

---

418 *Daily News*, December 22, 1933.

was time to move forward. The *Telegram* called on Newfoundland to "give of its best, loyally and resolutely" to bring back prosperity and self-government, a right it "relinquishes for the time being."[419] The *Telegram* was content, now that the Newfoundland legislation was passed in both London and St. John's, to proclaim Newfoundland safe "in the shelter and security of the arms of the Mother Country."[420]

The *Advocate* continued to be critical of the new form of government. Two months after Royal Assent had been given, and days after the Commission of Government was sworn in, the paper declared "Dictatorship and Oligarchy has been set up to rule the country for an indefinite period."[421]

Bishop William White reminded Anglicans in his Christmas letter that people's lives would improve only if residents and governments avoided going into debt. "We are losing sight of the immorality of using money we could not hope to repay," he wrote in the *Diocesan Magazine* of the circumstances that had led to the loss of responsible government, and Newfoundland was now "reaping the whirlwind." There was a lesson in this state of affairs for Anglicans, White intoned, "Halt while you have the time, for otherwise, ... either you or your children will reap a harvest of misery."[422]

With the constitutional question settled, Alderdice prepared to travel to London where he would discuss his role in the future government of Newfoundland. He was still prime minister, and in that position, he would meet the king and be honoured by Britain

---

419 *Evening Telegram*, December 22, 1933.

420 Ibid.

421 *Advocate*, February 23, 1934.

422 *Daily News*, December 23, 1933.

for having implemented Amulree's report without delay, and—more importantly as far as authorities in London were concerned—he did it without an election or referendum.

CHAPTER 13

The Alderdices Go to London

Two days after Christmas 1933, Fred and Harriet Alderdice and their daughter Doris were driven to the Furness and Withy pier in St. John's to begin a six-day journey to Liverpool. From there they would go to London, where they would meet the city's political elite and where Alderdice would receive details on how the new government of Newfoundland would function. The *Telegram* commiserated with Alderdice and the task he was setting out to accomplish. He was making the trip "under circumstances that cannot be regarded as pleasurable," the editorial offered, but "he has the satisfaction at least that the mess which has led to this situation is not of his making."[423]

Alderdice was carrying a letter from the Monroe Export Company, apparently requested the day before by him, concerning the financial crisis in Romania and the $800,000 worth of investments held there by Newfoundland businessmen, nearly half of them held by the Monroes and the Harveys. The previous

---

423 *Evening Telegram*, December 27, 1933.

year Romania had suspended pension and suppliers' payments in order to pay its international debt obligations. But with the world financial crisis deepening, the country was now suggesting that bondholders would get 20 per cent of their interest payment in cash in the first half of 1934, and the remainder in bonds. "Your idea is to get this capital out of its dormant position," the letter stated, and to have it "working for the good of the country's interest."[424] It may have been Alderdice's desire to get the British government involved in extricating the Newfoundland money, as a subsequent letter to him from Amulree Commission Secretary Clutterbuck stated, "you will be sending along papers about Roumanian Bonds."[425]

The Alderdices boarded the 406-foot SS *Nova Scotia*, which carried 15 first-class and 80 third-class passengers. The weather in

Government House, St. John's, ca. 1900. *ASC, Coll-137, 02.06.008*

---

424 The Rooms Provincial Archives of Newfoundland and Labrador, GN/8.250, Letter, Monroe Export Company to Alderdice, December 27, 1934.

425 Ibid., Letter, Alexander Clutterbuck to Alderdice, January 8, 1934.

St. John's was mild, but outside the Narrows the seas were up, pushed along by 30-mile-an-hour winds from the southeast. The trip across the Atlantic was slowed by fog but, just after New Year's Day, the Alderdices arrived in Liverpool. The UK Branch of the Empire Parliamentary Association had mailed Alderdice a voucher that entitled him to a half-fare rail trip to London. The prime minister had much on his mind during the train journey, likely including his own indecision about whether to accept the job as one of the three Newfoundland commissioners.

Governor David Murray Anderson, who had replaced Sir John Middleton as governor of Newfoundland in late 1932, had written to Edward Harding, the Permanent Undersecretary at the Dominions Office, before Alderdice left Newfoundland. He described Alderdice as "very tired mentally" after all that had happened in Newfoundland politics in the preceding months, adding that Alderdice was afraid the commissioners appointed from the UK might "adopt a superior and perhaps domineering attitude."[426]

The Alderdices settled into a suite at the high-class Rubens Hotel near the Royal Mews, a stone's throw from Buckingham Palace. The prime minister was deluged with invitations and meeting requests. The Secretary of State for War and former Lord Chancellor, Viscount Hailsham, wrote to request lunch; Middleton invited him to a talk on Newfoundland at the Royal Institute of International Affairs. Amulree sent a note from his home at St. Abbs, Berwickshire, to express hope that "things are moving satisfactorily in Newfoundland."[427] At the Rubens, the Alderdices

---

426 Neary, *Newfoundland in the North Atlantic World*, 45.

427 The Rooms Provincial Archives of Newfoundland and Labrador, MG/216, Letter, Amulree to Alderdice, January 3, 1934.

paid 50 shillings[428] a night. Alderdice was driven around London in a hired Daimler, which came with the "chauffeur Rose," and for that he was billed 10 guineas weekly,[429] a fee that increased if he travelled more than 250 miles in a week.

Alderdice's real business in London was to settle the details of the transfer of power in meetings at the Dominions Office. That involved meeting the key people involved in completing the details for the new government and understanding the new Newfoundland constitution. The morning after his arrival, Alderdice met

The Commission of Government takes office in St. John's, February 16, 1934. *The Rooms Provincial Archives of Newfoundland and Labrador, B4-137*

---

428 Close to Can$300 in 2014 value.

429 Worth 21 shillings, or slightly more than £1.

Dominions Secretary Thomas and was surprised at Thomas's knowledge of what had transpired in Newfoundland. A private meeting with Prime Minister MacDonald stretched on past its allocated time. Alderdice said he was impressed by MacDonald's "sympathy with Newfoundland in the commendable and determined effort of the people to bring the country back to solvency, [and MacDonald] was kind enough to tender a luncheon to him and Mrs. Alderdice [and] the principal ministers of the United Kingdom."[430]

A few days after arriving in London, Alderdice met two of his future colleagues, British-appointed commissioners John Hope Simpson and Thomas Lodge, at a lunch arranged by Harding. Alderdice was sufficiently impressed to approve of their appointments. In addition to discussing his own role in the new government, Alderdice wanted to obtain positions for four former Cabinet colleagues, a lingering issue since Cabinet had agreed to support Amulree's recommendations. In a letter to Amulree, Alderdice said that he "could not be certain of putting through the requisite legislation" if it was not possible "to assure [his] Ministers that their support of Government by Commission would not involve their being cast adrift."[431] The officials in London were strongly opposed to making such appointments or to any payments in lieu of appointments but decided not to spoil Alderdice's London trip. Alderdice would discover the disappointing answer once he was back in Newfoundland.[432]

Anderson had put Alderdice's name forward to be one of the Newfoundland commissioners but Alderdice apparently had

---

430 *Evening Telegram*, February 15, 1934.

431 Neary, *Newfoundland in the North Atlantic World*, 32.

432 Ibid., 46.

misgivings about taking on the job. Alderdice's letters to his friend William C. Job, who had managed the Job Brothers London office since 1925, have not survived, but Job's side of the exchange has. "My dear Fred," began Job's letter of January 4, 1934, "it would indeed be an unpatriotic Newfoundlander who would discourage such an appointment; your experience during the past few years must surely be necessary for the guidance of the Commission!"[433] As Job had served in the Legislative Council from 1909 to 1917, he was aware of the political consequences of turning down the offer. A successful businessman, he was also knowledgeable about Alderdice's own business interests, principally in Colonial Cordage Company. "Taking the cold business view," Job continued, "it seems clear your sons are well able to carry on the business." But he was concerned about the Newfoundland fishing industry, especially its reliance on credit being extended to fishermen: "I cannot help remembering your two uncles' cousins at all times for the credit that was to be issued. I know in some quarters in Newfoundland this part of the business has been carried on in a reckless manner the last few years." Job would be happy to recommend that Alderdice take the commissioner's job if he "thought [he] were keeping an eye on this part of the business ..." Job offered to call on Alderdice the following Monday and take him to the Hudson's Bay Company in London, where they could "look over some furs before lunch."

While in London, Alderdice received a copy of the 1933 Newfoundland High Commissioner's Office annual report. The office, then headed by Sir Edgar Bowring,[434] operated on a shoestring,

---

433 The Rooms Provincial Archives of Newfoundland and Labrador, MG/216.6, Letter, William C. Job to Alderdice, January 4, 1934.

434 *Daily News*, May 9, 1933. Bowring had accepted the role in the spring of 1933 and agreed to carry out the duties of High Commissioner without a salary.

and cost £1,996 that year compared to £139,241 for Canada's office, £55,624 for Australia's, and £38,334 for New Zealand's. Newfoundland's office employed five people, compared to 113 in the Canadian office, 92 in the Australian, and 78 in the New Zealand. At the end of the 1932 fiscal year, the Newfoundland office, facing an overdraft of just over £231, applied to the government in St. John's for additional funds. The application was rejected and the staff told to use whatever economies it could, and to solve the problem themselves. Officials, using "every effort" to cut spending, trimmed the overdraft by nearly half. A year later, the office remained £123 short. Bowring loaned £130 out his personal funds to cover the shortfall.[435]

During 1933, the High Commissioner's Office received 3,000 letters, and mailed 3,502; it sent 175 cables and telegrams and 49 parcels. The staff, though small in number, was expected to obtain tickets to various sites of interest for visiting Newfoundlanders, including admittance to the House of Lords and House of Commons galleries, the Guards' Chapel, the Royal Mint and Royal News, the Temple Church, and the Tower of London.[436] Alderdice was provided admittance cards to the House of Commons and its associated rooms on January 23 and he also had a pass to visit the House of Lords.

At least one Newfoundland journalist was keen to report on Alderdice's London visit. A week after Alderdice arrived in London, Albert Perlin sent a request for "about fifty words concerning any special development." Alderdice also had his own personal business to take care of. In the days before credit cards and travellers

---

435 The Rooms Provincial Archives of Newfoundland and Labrador, Office of the High Commissioner for Newfoundland, GN/8.250, Report for the year ended 31st December, 1933.

436 Ibid.

cheques, it was necessary for him to have the Bank of Nova Scotia in St. John's cable £250 to his account in London.

Alderdice's trip concluded with a farewell luncheon given by Thomas at the recently opened luxury Dorchester Hotel on Park Lane overlooking Hyde Park. Over a lunch of oysters, smoked salmon, grilled sole, and German and French wines, the Alderdices were joined by expatriate Newfoundlanders and senior British politicians. The Newfoundland guests included the former prime minister Lord Morris; High Commissioner Bowring; William Job; Mrs. J.S. Munn; and Sir Wilfred and Lady Grenfell. On the British side, Amulree was present, as was Clutterbuck; other guests included politicians who had previous relationships with either the Dominions or the Colonies Offices; also present were the Minister of Transport Sir Edward Grigg and MP Leslie-Hore Belisha, who had both taken part in the Newfoundland debate.

A day later, Alderdice was a guest of King George V at Sandringham, the royal estate more than two hours by train from London and the king's favourite home. Alderdice was suitably impressed by the king and by the surroundings. "[We] had a very pleasant conversation in private over a wide range of subjects," Alderdice told the *Telegram*, as "His Majesty recalled the time when as a midshipman he visited Newfoundland and engaged in fishing at Flat Bay Brook where he landed his first salmon." The king remembered the heat and mosquitoes but, in spite of it all, had had an enjoyable trip. As their meeting ended, he told Alderdice that "he would be watching the progress of the Commission Government with great interest."[437]

The details of the new governing body were complete by the time the Newfoundland delegation was seen off at Euston Station

---

437 *Daily News*, February 17, 1934.

in London by Prime Minister MacDonald, the Dominions Secretary, John Thomas, and other British dignitaries. The lord mayor bid the Alderdices, the Lodges, and Hope Simpsons farewell in Liverpool, as they boarded the SS *Montclare*, a 549-foot passenger ship owned by the Canadian Pacific Line, on February 2, bound for Halifax. In Halifax, they transferred to the SS *Silvia* for the trip to St. John's. In Halifax, reporters asked Hope Simpson for his impression of the job he was about to take on in Newfoundland. Ever the diplomat, he told them, "I cannot profitably say anything with regard to conditions in Newfoundland, as I have not yet visited the country ..."[438] He had talked extensively with Alderdice on the voyage across the Atlantic and was determined "to go to St. John's at once and ... commence work as soon as possible." The group arrived in St. John's on February 15, a day before the reading of the Letters Patent outlining the new form of government and the swearing-in of the six commissioners by the governor.

As the *Silvia* tied up at 7 a.m., photographers stood on the dock to capture the moment. The ship, decked out in flags, was opened up for an official boarding at 9:30 a.m. High-ranking local officials welcomed Alderdice and greeted the British commissioners. A delegation led by Puddester, and including Captain Robinson, who represented the governor, members of the Cabinet, the President of the Legislative Council, Commissioners Trentham and Howley, and Inspector General Hutchings of the Constabulary, all went on board. With the official greeting over, the UK commissioners and their wives rode to the Newfoundland Hotel and the suites where they would live while they were in Newfoundland.

The next day, one hundred years after Newfoundland was

438 *Evening Telegram*, February 14, 1934.

granted representative government, and less than two years after Alderdice was elected in a landslide victory, Alderdice and his Cabinet presented themselves before the governor and resigned as ministers of the Crown. Shortly afterward, the Speaker of the House of Assembly and the President of the Legislative Council arrived and relinquished their positions. Responsible government, bitterly fought for through the late 1840s and early 1850s, had ended. There was one more formality: the adoption of the constitution and the swearing-in of the new government. This was carried out with much ceremony at the Newfoundland Hotel on February 16. Those who had been given special invitations to the event were seated in the hotel ballroom. Outside, at 2:55 p.m., Governor Anderson and his wife arrived from Government House to a Guard of Honour comprised of the Constabulary, the GVWA, and the CLB Band. At the entrance to the hotel ballroom, the governor was met by Chief Justice William Horwood, the six commissioners, and Deputy Secretary of State Arthur Mews. They walked slowly to the dais and took their seats, which had been decided weeks before in London. Anderson called on Mews to read the Letters Patent proclaiming the new constitution, and the governor signed the Proclamation. Anderson gave a short speech and read a message from the Dominions Secretary.

Hope Simpson and Alderdice took the stage. Alderdice praised the British commissioners as "men of outstanding ability and wide and varied experience" whose "selection attests to their eminent suitability for the responsibility and important work in which they are about to engage."[439] He recounted how the king had told him he would watch with "sympathetic interest" what was happening in Newfoundland and expressed his own hope

---

439 *Daily News*, February 17, 1934.

that the people would rally around the Commission of Government, as no government "can hope to improve the condition of a country unless it is supported by public opinion and reaffirmed by the cooperation of the people." Alderdice reaffirmed his own support for the withdrawal of responsible government and said the new administration would be "free from the distracting elements of political expediency and party interests ..., [and] will be devoted solely to the implementing of a programme of expansion of the country's industries, the broader development of its trade and commerce and the placing of its financial fabric upon a firm and lasting foundation."[440]

The *Daily News* called it a "solemn ceremony, the final act in the relinquishment of self-government by Newfoundland." It acknowledged that "it may have different reactions in different minds," but concluded there was an undeniable lesson for "the younger generation [for it brought] a full realization that if democracy brings privileges it brings even greater responsibilities."[441] The *Telegram* wrote that Newfoundland "has turned over the pages that in recent years have recorded much that has been distressing and humiliating ... the work that lies ahead is bound to prove onerous. It will call for sacrifice."[442]

After the ceremony, the commissioners went to Government House, where Anderson administered the oath of office. After that, a Gazette Extraordinary was issued to give official public notice of the new constitution.

As the final, visible sign that responsible government was indeed over, contractor Charles Udle and his crew moved into the

---

440 Ibid.

441 Ibid.

442 *Evening Telegram*, February 16, 1934.

Colonial Building and began converting the House of Assembly and the Legislative Council Chambers into office space for the new Department of Natural Resources, which included fisheries, agriculture, and forestry. The Speaker's Office and members' rooms were taken over by the commissioner and his staff. The chamber, which had rung with debate and intrigue for 80 years, was being prepared for department staff. The Legislative Council was renovated for marine and fisheries officials, the Codfish Exportation Board took over the second floor, and the Secretary of Agriculture set up shop in the basement.

CHAPTER 14

The End

Alderdice, a tired man by the time he returned to Newfoundland for the inauguration of the Commission of Government, was chosen vice-chair of the Commission, a position that befitted his former role as Newfoundland's prime minister. He knew that his battle to arrange employment for some of his ex-Cabinet ministers was yet to come—although it didn't amount to much of a battle. Just as he refused to press London for better conditions in the wake of the Amulree Report, Alderdice capitulated to the strident British position that a campaign to employ ex-ministers might be portrayed in the British Parliament as "blackmail" and viewed "unfavourably" by the new government in Newfoundland. The incident, though, "left him thoroughly disillusioned."[443] After being sworn in to his $5,000-a-year job as Commissioner for Home Affairs and Education, Alderdice took a three-month leave of absence.

A key recommendation of the Amulree Report was the conversion of Newfoundland's bond to 3 per cent interest, a reduction of at least two percentage points from the interest rates that

---

443 Neary, *Newfoundland in the North Atlantic World*, 50.

crippled the previous government. The effect on the bottom line in St. John's was immediate—it allowed the Commission of Government to allocate $3,115,000 for interest expenses, a reduction of $2,100,000 from 1933. Part of the Amulree recommendations was that London would cover shortfalls in the Newfoundland budget until at least 1936; in 1934, that was estimated to be $2,192,500, an amount slightly higher than the savings from reduced interest charges. By the time the accounts were settled in 1935, Newfoundland required only $1,743,173 to cover the shortfall, but the safety net was nevertheless in place. The Commission also borrowed $1,167,695 from the Colonial Development Fund, set up in 1929 by Britain to deliver foreign aid to its colonies and dependencies. Nearly half of that amount was used to build 320 fishing boats, including 20 schooners for the Labrador fishery. Two hundred thousand dollars was used to rehabilitate Newfoundland's roads, and $300,000 to improve railway and wharfage at Port aux Basques for the shipment of newsprint.

As Home Affairs Secretary, Alderdice was responsible for education. One of the Commission's first acts was to allocate an increase of $207,000, most of which was used to increase teachers' salaries. Despite this good news, the education system would become an early and continuing source of friction between Alderdice and the British commissioners.

In a letter to his daughter Greta in August 1934, less than six months after the new government took office, Hope Simpson despaired that every community demanded a denominational school and that Alderdice was doing little as Home Affairs Secretary to dissuade them of that notion. "He has done nothing for the past five months," Hope Simpson complained, adding that Alderdice's department was causing the British commissioners "great anxiety."[444] A year later, nothing had improved either in the relationship between Hope Simpson and Alderdice, or in the education system. "The root problem [in Newfoundland] is lack of education," Hope Simpson complained to Greta. Newfoundland needed a state-run system, not one run by the churches, but Alderdice would not allow it. Hope Simpson told his daughter that the British commissioners "have inserted the thin edge of the wedge" to change things, but Alderdice "is a nervous person and will not apply the hammer except with gentle taps, and then only when his ruthless UK Commissioners become impatient and drive him to it."[445]

Education was a continuing source of consternation for the Hope Simpsons. Hope Simpson lamented in a letter to his son Ian and daughter-in-law Sheila, in April 1936, about his wish that "one of [the British commissioners] had education. This is where drastic reform is needed most, and it will not happen under a Newfoundland Commissioner." He concluded: "things will not commence to progress until we get rid of this damnable denominational education."[446] Hope Simpson's wife, Quita, who, early in her stay in Newfoundland, had determined St. John's to be "just a dirty foul-smelling slum," shared her husband's concerns. "Of course, education is not Daddy's department," she wrote to Greta in July 1936, "it was Mr. Alderdice's and he did nothing."[447]

The best the Commission could do was make administrative changes in the Education Act, ending weeks of "street gossip and rumour" of more substantial and drastic change that would see

---

444 Neary, ed., *White Tie and Decorations*, 114.

445 Ibid., 244–45, Letter, Simpson to Greta, October 27, 1935.

446 Ibid., 287, Letter, Simpson to Ian and Sheila, April 15, 1936.

447 Ibid., 331, Letter, Quita to Greta, July 30, 1936.

the role of the churches diminished. Perlin reported in the *Observer's Weekly* that the changes were designed to "centralize control, lay the way open for all-round improvement of general education policy."[448] The chief outcome as far as Alderdice and the other two Newfoundland commissioners were concerned was that denominational control over education remained firmly in place.

The Commission restored morale in the public service by increasing pay and reorganizing the structure of the government along British lines. The Newfoundland Ranger Force was set up and became an extension of the government in all areas of Newfoundland, incorporating the roles of police officer, warden, social worker, customs officer, and any other job that was necessary. What did not change was the state of Newfoundland's economy, and that led to more violence in St. John's in May 1935.

The 1935 disturbance arose again out of residents' discontent with the dole payment and their inability to properly clothe themselves and heat their homes. The Commission government added cabbage and turnips to the dole order after a demonstration by 1,000 unemployed in February. That was not enough. On May 10 another large crowd of unemployed marched to the Colonial Building and clashed with police. That night they marched through the city, and smashed windows. Four were arrested, but were found not guilty.[449] The disturbances were not on the scale of those in 1932, yet they were unnerving for the governor and the Commission. A public meeting in St. John's in late October 1935

---

448 *Observer's Weekly*, March 14, 1935.

449 Carmelita McGrath and Kathryn Welbourne, "Riots and Reports: A Time of Change," in *Desperate Measures: The Great Depression in Newfoundland and Labrador*, Newfoundland and Labrador Adult Basic Education Social History series, Book 4, http://en.copian.ca/library/learning/social/book4/book4.pdf.

passed a resolution that called for the abolition of the Commis-sion and a return to responsible government. This motion was approved at public meetings in Placentia and Conception bays during the winter months.[450] The uneasiness pervasive in St. John's drove a further wedge between the Newfoundland com-missioners and their British colleagues.

Justice Commissioner William R. Howley, a Newfoundlander, made his dissatisfaction with the British commissioners known during a trip to London in December 1935. "The Newfoundland members do not feel that their views are really sought," he told the Dominions Office, arguing that this "was getting known to the public outside [and] derogating from the authority of the Admin-istration."[451] The lightning rod for Howley's complaint may have been "energetic, articulate and intellectually arrogant"[452] Com-missioner Thomas Lodge. Lodge, argued Howley, "was taking advantage of the Commission's weaknesses to urge changes in both [personnel and structure]." Lodge had devised an amended constitutional structure that would empower the governor and place the Newfoundland commissioners in advisory, rather than executive, positions. But British officials would not allow Com-mission in-fighting to become the story out of Newfoundland. Their first step to end Lodge's bullying was to replace the pliant Anderson with the no-nonsense Vice-Admiral Sir Humphrey Walwyn. The new governor detected that Lodge wanted a stronger position for himself in Newfoundland. Walwyn forwarded Lodge's brief for a new constitutional structure to the Dominions Office, but added a personal note. Lodge "is not wanted out here

---

450 Noel, *Politics in Newfoundland*, 227–43.

451 Ibid.

452 Ibid.

in that capacity," Walwyn wrote, "because of his inherent rudeness to people with a lower intelligence than himself!"[453] The Dominions Office did not want further trouble in Newfoundland: "it is essential in practice that everything should be done to raise the status of the Newfoundland members in the eyes of the public."[454] In the spring of 1937, three years after his arrival in Newfoundland, Lodge was out as a commissioner. The Dominions Office did not renew his appointment.

The British commissioners living in the Newfoundland Hotel formed a compact with officials brought over from London to administer Newfoundland.[455] Despite the tension that existed between them and their Newfoundland colleagues, the British were forced to socialize with the Newfoundlanders and with the St. John's mercantile elite. Hope Simpson regarded the merchants with disdain and distrust. As he wrote his daughter three months into the job: "They dislike me & they dislike the Commission of Government, because our main interest is prosperity among the common folk."[456] Concern for these common folk also put Hope Simpson at odds with Alderdice, as he recounted in a letter after a dinner at Charles Harvey's home in late September 1935. The dinner was attended by the usual collection of St. John's businessmen, including Sir Edgar Bowring and Herbert Outerbridge. Hope Simpson talked about the "appalling conditions on the island" and was reminded by Alderdice that "we U.K. commissioners should give up trying to raise the standard of living ... we only

---

453 Ibid.

454 Ibid.

455 Ibid.

456 Neary, *White Tie and Decorations*, Letter, Simpson to Greta, May 13, 1934, 87.

make the people discontented."[457]

The Commission, which had began in such hopeful circumstances, became mired in internal bickering and, worse, was ineffective in pushing back the economic problems that engulfed Newfoundland and its people. The number of people on relief dropped to under 32,000 in 1934 and 1935[458] from a high of 70,000 in the winter of 1932, but would increase to more than 38,000 in 1936. It would remain stubbornly high until the first year of World War II when the US military arrived in Newfoundland and employed thousands of Newfoundlanders at its bases in St. John's, Argentia, Stephenville, and Goose Bay.

At the end of the first two years of the Commission, conditions were a long way from the optimistic picture Alderdice had painted in the dying days of responsible government. In his opening speech to the legislature during the debate to adopt Amulree's plan, Alderdice said that Newfoundland stood to gain substantially: "not one man in five hundred will know the difference except that he will see prosperity restored to the country."[459]

These words rang hollow in 1935, and while the St. John's dailies remained supportive of the Commission of Government, the public heard other voices that advocated change. One of them was Albert Perlin, who in 1919 had began his career as a reporter with the *Telegram*, which continued through to the early 1930s with his "Pepys behind the Scenes" and "Topics of the Times" columns. In 1934, Perlin started the newsmagazine *Observer's Weekly*, intended to keep people apprised of the activities of the Commission of Government. In late November 1935, "with half

457 Ibid., Letter, Simpson to Betty, September 25, 1935, 222.

458 Noel, *Politics in Newfoundland*, 227–43.

459 Ibid.

the Commission, including two-thirds of the English representation, in London," Perlin argued that it was time to overhaul the way the Commission operated. Perlin was critical of the Commission on several fronts: it implemented "the most definite recommendations of the Amulree Report" without assessing "to what extent they were wise." He did credit the commissioners, especially the English representatives, with acknowledging that the government was on the wrong path, and concluded that they were "now undertaking enterprises … which should have been initiated eighteen months ago."[460] Overall, however, Perlin viewed the Commission as a dysfunctional government, with commissioners acting as individuals, jealously protecting their own departments to the detriment of the entire government. He insisted that it was time to put a businessman at the head of the Commission, who "must be above all department heads, with the authority to supervise the workings and policies of all departments."[461]

Perlin did not name who he had in mind for the job, but his criticism fit into the broader narrative that had begun to emerge in St. John's: the Commission was doing little to improve Newfoundland's economy. Noel argues that the English commissioners, in particular, seemed "less certain" than Amulree that the "cod-fishery has been, and must continue to be, the mainstay of the island."[462] "The forceful Thomas Lodge," in the absence of an overall plan to rebuild the Newfoundland economy, had been able to convince the Commission to agree to a scheme that resettled unemployed St. John's residents to a life of farming in Markland. The scheme was later abandoned, but not before it placed "a sufficient

---

460 *Observer's Weekly*, November 15, 1935.

461 Ibid.

462 Noel, *Politics in Newfoundland*, 227–43.

drain on the Commission's finances to render impossible any major reforms in the structure of the fishery ..."[463]

Perhaps it was fatigue, or his Conservative heart, or a combination of both, but Alderdice did not seem to have the motivation to find new ideas to restructure or rebuild the Newfoundland economy. As prime minister, he had frequently spoken of the fishery as Newfoundland's main industry, but as a commissioner he possessed little of the dash and energy that the new job required. In the middle of March 1934, while Commissioners Hope Simpson, Lodge, and Puddester toured the deficit-ridden railway line, Alderdice "was compelled to rest in bed following his strenuous trip abroad," according to Perlin. Alderdice broke his rest during that period to chair a public meeting at the Casino Theatre, but was again ordered to bed "to complete a rest cure." Perlin visited Alderdice on May 26; he was "much improved in appearance, albeit still under doctor's orders and must take much rest."[464]

Alderdice, at home with his family at Park Place on Sunday evening, February 23, 1936, sat by the radio listening to the broadcast of the British and Foreign Bible Society from Pitts Memorial Hall, the assembly hall for the United and Presbyterian Holloway School. The "crowded gathering" at the Hall included Governor and Lady Walwyn, and the event was broadcast on radio station VOWR. The Wesley Church Choir opened with William How's hymn "O Word of God Incarnate." Sometime during the broadcast, Alderdice suffered a stroke. His doctor was called immediately, but Alderdice did not regain consciousness. He died at 6 a.m. February 26, two and a half days after the stroke.

The Alderdice family agreed to a state funeral at St. Thomas'

---

463 Ibid.
464 *Observer's Weekly*, May 1935.

Anglican Church, where Fred and Harriett had been married 36 years earlier. The funeral procession, led by the Boy Scouts, the CLB, the GWVA, and the Constabulary, started at the Alderdice home and wound its way along streets lined with people on both sides. Harriett and the Alderdice children came behind the hearse, followed by Privy Councillors, the Supreme Court judges, members of the Commission of Government, representatives of foreign governments, ex-members of the Legislative Council and House of Assembly, the mayor and councillors of St. John's, members of the Board of Trade, employees of Alderdice's Colonial Cordage Company, and private citizens. The funeral service was led by seven Church of England ministers, including five Canons and the Lord Bishop of Newfoundland. The Alderdice family requested the singing of Isaac Watts's "When I Survey the Wondrous Cross." Alderdice was buried in the Church of England cemetery on Forest Road.

The man who was rescued from the uncertainties of life in 1886 Belfast by his uncle in St. John's and who rose through the city's business and mercantile elites to become Newfoundland's last prime minister was gone. The St. John's papers portrayed his life as tragic but heroic, caught between his physical disabilities and the intractable economic and fiscal challenges of his prime ministership.

"It was a courageous act to assume the burdens of the premiership at a time when national credit had been exhausted," wrote the *Daily News*, "and after nearly eighteen months of intolerable mental and physical strain, the choice was offered between default … and the temporary abdication of responsible government." Of his decision not to hold the referendum he had promised during the 1932 campaign, the paper concluded, "there was little time for consideration, no time at all for a plebiscite" on the Amulree recommendations. In any event, the paper wrote, such a vote among the population was likely to do more harm than good: "National pride in complete self-determination may often obscure realities and create opposition to a step definitely to the popular advantage."[465]

Questions linger about Alderdice's time as prime minister of Newfoundland and the extent to which his hand was forced in accepting Amulree's report—and conversely, whether a stouter defence of Newfoundland and responsible government would have extracted a better offer from London. Certain factors conspired against a spirited attack on Amulree's recommendations, chief among them Alderdice's affection for, and loyalty to, the British Empire, a sentiment that was presented in many of his speeches about Newfoundland's predicament and did not waver even as he failed to get British orders for Bell Island ore in the wake of the 1932 Imperial Conference in Ottawa. Alderdice was British through and through.

Alderdice held a narrow view of the world, developed through a lifetime in business. In that world, the bottom line had to be taken care of, and when Britain undertook to meet Newfoundland's fiscal needs with its offer in the early fall of 1933, that was what mattered to Alderdice. His election promise to get the approval of people before implementing a commission of government was secondary, and easily explained away or ignored. Alderdice was a democratically elected leader with little professed appreciation for the value of a democracy, and the implications of losing it. Indeed, in the public debate in Newfoundland after Amulree, the *Advocate*, Coaker, and Liberal leader Gordon Bradley stood out for defending the right of the people to choose their own government.

Alderdice had displayed a large measure of political naivete,

465 *Daily News*, February 26, 1936.

evident in his plan to partially default in the fall of 1932. In the face of the strong pushback from the Dominions Office, Alderdice quickly backed down. No evidence indicates that he considered exploiting London's argument that no British government had ever defaulted, when in fact the government at Westminster suspended payment on its World War I debt to the US after 1932, and has never repaid the balance. Alderdice might also have benefited from pushing the Dominions Office to determine how far it would go to avoid having Newfoundland default, and whether under such circumstances Newfoundland could retain control of its government. A year later, the British would engineer their own version of partial default, by converting Newfoundland's debt to British-backed debt and unilaterally reducing Newfoundland's interest rates on debt by about 2 per cent.

Alderdice was a man of his class. He reflected the deeply held beliefs and instincts of the St. John's mercantile elite, many of whom believed responsible government should never have been granted to Newfoundland. Theirs was a world of control, control over the price fishermen were paid for their catch, and control over their thousands of employees in the shops and offices of St. John's—a group with significant influence over public affairs. It is unlikely that there was any talk in the parlours of the homes of the leading citizens of the city about keeping responsible government at any cost, especially if it meant risking their own investments or if it curtailed their ability to raise credit. In the various debates in the House of Assembly and the Legislative Council, leading government supporters, including Alderdice, made it abundantly clear that responsible government had been a failure, and more than that, a mistake.

If responsible government was a failure and a mistake, who was to blame? Amulree's conclusion that a rest from politics was the only cure for a political system that had become corrupt is too easy a diagnosis. Newfoundland's path in 1933-34 might have been avoided with sound decision-making in the four or five years leading up to the Great Depression. During this period, Newfoundland's main exports of fish, paper, and iron ore were strong. Yet, the government, led by Walter Monroe, borrowed nearly $20 million from 1924 to 1928 and increased Newfoundland's debt to $85 million. Even as he went to the markets and borrowed more money, Monroe further enriched the upper classes by abolishing income tax, a major source of government revenue. He also eliminated the Profits Tax on business, leading his finance minister, John Crosbie, to conclude that that measure would cost the Newfoundland Treasury more than $1 million, an amount that surpassed the new tariffs that the government had placed on goods such as beef, flour, pork, and gasoline. Crosbie predicted bankruptcy was looming for Newfoundland, the result, he felt, of declining revenue and increasing spending:

> After my two years' experience in office I am fully convinced that the country is going back to pre-war revenue while I am just as sure that expenditure is steadily marching ahead with only one result for the Colony.[466]

Monroe's failure to control costs in a growing economy and the decision to give up substantial revenue by eliminating income

---

466 John Perlin personal papers, St. John's, Letter, John C. Crosbie to Prime Minister Walter Stanley Monroe, December 21, 1926. Crosbie wrote the letter days before Christmas, but delayed delivering it. He wrote: "I feel like delivering this letter to you to-day, but remembering how near Christmas it is, I have on second thought decided to let Christmas Day pass before sending it."

tax and the profits tax took away some of the flexibility New-foundland would need to grapple with the economic and fiscal problems of the early 1930s. Monroe had come to power with a plan to clean up government and politics after the scandals involving Squires. Yet, he had also come to realize that "you can't run a Government as a private business."[467] He borrowed to cover the previous year's deficits, build roads, purchase a new ferry for the crossing to Nova Scotia, and upgrade the railroad. He found that "retrenchment was always easier to promise in a campaign than to effect in office," according to Patrick O'Flaherty, and "he kept on spending and borrowing when his instincts told him what was needed was severe retrenchment."[468]

In the decades since Alderdice's prime ministership, writers and historians have tried to understand the factors that led to Confederation with Canada in 1949. There is ample proof that both Canada and Britain eased the way toward the union of British North America. But like Amulree's conclusion, that too is an over-simplification. Newfoundland was in control of its own government for nearly eight decades after the granting of responsible government in 1855. Alliances, coalitions, and parties of Newfoundlanders—fishermen, businessmen, lawyers, and doctors—made the laws and borrowed and spent on behalf of their countrymen. They led Newfoundland down the path from which it could not extricate itself in 1933. It was the leaders from these classes who agreed to the deal with Britain in late 1932 to begin the Amulree Commission; it was this group that promised to consult the people on the constitutional future of Newfoundland, but chose not to.

And of course, they might have felt, why should they? Alderdice

---

467 O'Flaherty, *Lost Country*, 343.
468 Ibid., 344.

and the UNP had complete control of the legislature after their landslide win in 1932. The absence of a real debate on Amulree's report in Newfoundland in November 1933 paved the way for the Parliament at Westminster to give its blessing to the report. Newfoundland had accepted an open-ended suspension of its government without a fight, and without any consideration that the citizens might one day want to resume running their own affairs. That said, Newfoundland politicians did believe they had a way out; that if they wanted to resume self-government, all they would have to do is ask the government in Westminster to allow it to happen.

Much of the historical and political analysis of the period between 1934 and 1949 focuses on the intrigue surrounding Confederation. Many Newfoundland writers place the blame on Canada and Britain for engineering the union between Newfoundland and Canada. Newfoundland literature, art, and music portrays rough and rugged individualism and shows Newfoundlanders as a people ready to take on the interlopers who would interfere with a community and its strong sense of belonging and purpose. It is difficult to accept that the mythology does not always mesh with the reality.

Blaming Canada and Britain for Confederation ignores the role played by Newfoundland leaders in the years leading up to 1934, when the conditions were put in place that made Confederation possible. O'Flaherty points to the succession of leaders, including Monroe, who "lacked … faith" in "Newfoundland's future as an independent country."[469] That point was borne out in the debate around the conclusions of the Amulree Report and the willingness to accept the loss of responsible government. During that debate, Alderdice and senior politicians in the Legislative Council said they believed that self-government was a mistake.

---

469 Ibid.

The two St. John's dailies held the same view. The Newfoundland mercantile community, with its destructive practices in buying and selling fish, and its exploitive credit system, played a significant role in stymieing the modernization of the fishing industry and development of communities.

What happened after 1934 had an air of inevitability. Those who wanted a return to responsible government after they saw the appointed Commission of Government in action were the ones who had given it away in a wave of euphoric release in 1933. Those opposed to self-government were rejecting a return to the ruling classes of pre-Commission days. Having responsible government back, the thinking went, would reward the political elites who would dispense electoral favours, while keeping the structure of the Newfoundland economy as it had been for two centuries. Fishermen would continue to be subjugated to the will of the merchants, their catch undervalued, and their return diminished.

Newfoundland, despite the onerous weight placed on its finances through its war and railway debt, had the chance, on several occasions, to find its own way, and to attempt to become a functioning, independent country. That dream would still have been a long shot given the underdevelopment of its infrastructure, the state of its main industry, the fishery, and the fragile state of its finances. But as long as Newfoundlanders controlled their own political and constitutional destiny, that chance would have existed. The events of 1932 and 1933 extinguished that dream. The conditions were created by Newfoundlanders themselves, including people who had a dim view of their own people and the value that self-government provided. That attitude was reflected in Alderdice's decision not to consult the public on the recommendation to place Newfoundland under a Commission of Government: "No action will be taken that does not first have the consent of the people,"[470] he had stated during the election campaign.

The Alderdice government, with two and a half years left in its mandate, relinquished political control with virtually no public debate. The Balfour Declaration of 1926, with its unambiguous direction that the Dominions, including Newfoundland, were to be autonomous, did not resonate with Alderdice and his government.[471] Their capitulation in the face of serious financial problems in late 1933 put Newfoundland in the care of an appointed bureaucratic organization. In doing so, Alderdice handed over control of the future of Newfoundland's constitutional status to politicians and their officials in London.

---

470 *Alderdice Manifesto*, 14.

471 Neither did it resonate with Walter S. Monroe, who attended the 1926 Imperial Conference as prime minister of Newfoundland. He told the Newfoundland legislature on May 11, 1927, "we are now an autonomous community equal in Status with any other Dominion of the British Empire. We did not ask for it, nor did we want it, and we did not throw our hats in the air when we go it. It is of no value to us." *Proceedings*, May 11, 1927, 17.

ACKNOWLEDGEMENTS

The idea for this book came during a class at Memorial University in the winter of 1977. Dr. Jim Hiller led us on a spellbinding tour of Newfoundland history, with stories about the scoundrels and scandals hatched during nearly a century of self-government.

Of all the names and dates and changes in government, one thing struck me: Newfoundland had once been a country and had given it up. I was intrigued, and I told myself that one day I would find out why, and perhaps write a book about it. About five years ago, I decided it was time to begin exploring the topic.

This book would not have been possible without the many Newfoundland history and political science courses offered at Memorial. Neither could it be possible without the Centre for Newfoundland Studies and the Archives and Special Collections at the Queen Elizabeth II Library and the Provincial Archives of Newfoundland and Labrador at the Rooms. The people at those institutions are themselves provincial treasures.

Along the way, some wonderful people gave me a hand. Jim Hiller kindly read an early copy of the manuscript and offered sound advice. Bert Riggs and Linda White answered questions and dug for more material, and then answered even more questions.

My former colleague Jay Callanan read an early iteration, and made valuable suggestions. I was also encouraged by a group of history aficionados, known as the Holyrood History Group, which includes Ron Whelan, Kevin Melvin, Gerry Squires, Bruce Woodland, Bob Woodland, Tom Burke, Tom Dawe, Jean Pierre Andrieux, Aidan Maloney, and Melvin Baker. Mel read a near-finished manuscript and steered me away from danger spots.

This book would not have been possible without the people at Boulder Publications. Gavin Will believed in the project from the start, and started the ball rolling. Stephanie Porter showed great patience and tact as we edited and re-edited. She helped shape the narrative into a more readable book, and I am grateful. Iona Bulgin went through the text and the footnotes with great skill, and a fine-toothed comb! The book is the better for it.

I must also thank the people who documented the story of Newfoundland's political life through the newspapers of the day, and those who saved and stored the government documents that provide an account of the time. My only regret is that so few politicians saved their personal papers, and because of that, we are cheated of their unique perspective of those days and the events that led to the loss of parliamentary democracy in Newfoundland.

Regardless of the gaps I've identified with personal accounts and other material, I have attempted to tell the story of a tumultuous time in Newfoundland history through a narrative that I hope challenges us to think about that period in a new way.

Doug Letto
Paradise, August 2014

ABOUT THE AUTHOR

Doug Letto's passion for history and politics matured during his undergraduate studies at Memorial University, after which he completed a Masters degree in political science. For more than three decades, he was one of Newfoundland and Labrador's most familiar faces as a CBC television political reporter, co-anchor of *Here & Now*, and producer. During that time, Letto authored a best-selling book on the Smallwood government's industrialization program. *Chocolate Bars and Rubber Boots* chronicled the foolhardy investment of scarce government funds in factories that produced ballet shoes, English chocolate, and rubber boots that fell apart. *Newfoundland's Last Prime Minister* is his fourth book.